Praise for *Rekindle Y*

"If you've ever wondered how to create the [ ]
for your alarm clock to buzz so you can ge[ ]
rings you skip gleefully to the parking lot, ecstatic about the difference you made,
look no further. In *Rekindle Your Professional Fire,* Mike Anderson has brought
those conditions to life. There's a recipe in here, and like most recipes, if you tinker
with it a little bit to make it your own, you can flourish . . . so that your students can
do the same."

—**Pete Hall**, former school principal and author of *Always Strive to Be a Better You*

"Far too often, teachers are fearful, burned out, overly exhausted, and feeling
stuck. Mike Anderson has written a book that's chock-full of gems for cultivating
curiosity, healthy habits, play, and passion—all in service of becoming well-
balanced, healthier teachers. This is one of those grab and go, tab and mark up sort
of reads that's easy to digest and practical, too."

—**Nawal Qarooni**, literacy consultant, author,
and educator with NQC Literacy

"Mike Anderson offers a hopeful message that we all need to hear now more than
ever: under the right conditions, teaching can be more than just a job; it can be
a *great, life-giving profession*. With lively prose and compelling personal stories,
Anderson deftly weaves together research and life lessons into practical, everyday
shifts in professional practice and habits of mind that teachers can use right away
to do more than survive, but actually thrive in their classrooms and along the way,
rekindle their joy of teaching."

—**Bryan Goodwin**, president and CEO of McREL International
and author of *The New Classroom Instruction That Works*

"As a seasoned teacher who's experienced bouts of teacher guilt and fatigue, I found
that this book spoke to me. New teachers: Read this book to begin these practices
early on in your career so they become habits. Veteran teachers: Read this book
as a check-in tool to both adjust and reaffirm your thinking. Administrators: Read
this book to gain insight into what your staff may be thinking and feeling but are
too afraid to say out loud. Anderson's simple tips are manageable, transcend the
classroom, and will have you saying, 'Why didn't I think of that?'"

—**Lindsey Bickford**, classroom teacher, Pittsfield, New Hampshire

"This book provides some great strategies to restore the joy that is at the center of
our work. Mike Anderson's blend of advice and research-based practices are a recipe
for healthy restoration and rejuvenation that every and any educator can follow."

—**Marlene M. Silano**, assistant superintendent,
Cheshire Public Schools, Cheshire, Connecticut

"Most professional books focus on how you should teach. Mike Anderson's *Rekindle Your Professional Fire* is about how to create the kind of life around your teaching that will help you stay fulfilled and full of passion for teaching. Mike is the wise, empathetic, and practical mentor you need to create a well-balanced teaching life."

—**Carl Anderson**, literacy consultant and co-author of
How to Become a Better Writing Teacher

"As educators, we've all felt overwhelmed at times, where the purpose behind our teaching gets blurred. But fear not! In Mike Anderson's book, rediscover your true calling in education. Through relatable stories and actionable tips, it guides us in self-care and reigniting our spark for teaching. Discover how the same six key intrinsic motivators we use with students can also empower our professional lives. Whether you're a teacher or administrator, these strategies are invaluable. Let this resource be our guide to reclaiming our best self in the classroom."

—**Piesesha Hartiyana**, curriculum specialist at
HighScope Indonesia Institute, Jakarta, Indonesia

"As a guidance counselor working with behaviorally and academically at-risk students for the past 18 years, sometimes I reflect, especially during the more challenging weeks, on how I've made it this far. Mike Anderson's book offers practical advice and easy-to-implement strategies on developing habits that will strengthen, revitalize, and ultimately prolong the career of any educator who is feeling burned out and out-of-balance. I would highly recommend this book."

—**James Lopez**, MEd, Casa Blanca Community School,
Bapchule, Arizona

"Mike Anderson has written another inspiring and strategy-rich book for those determined to prosper as educators. He puts into words what most of us don't have the time or energy or skill to articulate: the work is hard, often not in our control, *and* we are still in this for the joy and pride we want for ourselves and our students. He rekindles our sense of competence and purpose by offering an incredible array of uncomplicated strategies we can build into our days. It would be impossible to read this book and not be underlining and circling ideas to try. Warning: if you are cynical, frustrated, and burned out, and want to stay that way, this book is not for you."

—**Jeffrey Benson**, author of *Hacking School Discipline Together*

"Mike Anderson once again delivers a book needed by our profession. His latest is a collection of applicable wisdom that has been expertly curated, interpreted, and applied to our profession. Mike's conversational delivery of this practical, relevant wisdom is certain to engage educators of all experience levels. From first-year teachers to seasoned principals, this should be required reading for all educators."

—**Ed Joyce**, principal, Ross A. Lurgio Middle School,
Bedford, New Hampshire

REKINDLE YOUR PROFESSIONAL FIRE

Also by Mike Anderson

Tackling the Motivation Crisis:
How to Activate Student Learning Without Behavior Charts,
Pizza Parties, or Other Hard-to-Quit Incentive Systems

What We Say and How We Say It Matter:
Teacher Talk That Improves Student Learning and Behavior

Learning to Choose, Choosing to Learn:
The Key to Student Motivation and Achievement

The Well-Balanced Teacher:
How to Work Smarter and Stay Sane Inside the Classroom and Out

Teacher Talk That Matters
(Quick Reference Guide)

MIKE ANDERSON

REKINDLE YOUR PROFESSIONAL FIRE

Powerful Habits for Becoming a More Well-Balanced Teacher

ascd

Arlington, Virginia USA

2800 Shirlington Road, Suite 1001 • Arlington, VA 22206 USA
Phone: 800-933-2723 or 703-578-9600 • Fax: 703-575-5400
Website: www.ascd.org • Email: member@ascd.org
Author guidelines: www.ascd.org/write

Richard Culatta, *Chief Executive Officer;* Anthony Rebora, Chief Content Officer; Genny Ostertag, *Managing Director, Book Acquisitions & Editing;* Mary Beth Nielsen, *Director, Book Editing;* Liz Wegner, *Editor;* Thomas Lytle, *Creative Director;* Donald Ely, *Art Director;* Lisa Hill, *Graphic Designer;* Cynthia Stock, *Typesetter;* Kelly Marshall, *Production Manager;* Shajuan Martin, *E-Publishing Specialist;* Kathryn Oliver, *Creative Project Manager*

PAPERBACK ISBN: 978-1-4166-3303-7   ASCD product #124027
PDF EBOOK ISBN: 978-1-4166-3304-4; see Books in Print for other formats.
Quantity discounts are available: email programteam@ascd.org or call 800-933-2723, ext. 5773, or 703-575-5773. For desk copies, go to www.ascd.org/deskcopy.

ASCD Member Book No. FY24-5 (Jul 2024 PSI+). ASCD Member Books mail to Premium (P), Select (S), and Institutional Plus (I+) members on this schedule: Jan, PSI+; Feb, P; Apr, PSI+; May, P; Jul, PSI+; Aug, P; Sep, PSI+; Nov, PSI+; Dec, P. For current details on membership, see www.ascd.org/membership.

Library of Congress Cataloging-in-Publication Data

Names: Anderson, Mike, 1971– author.
Title: Rekindle your professional fire : powerful habits for becoming a more well-balanced teacher / Mike Anderson.
Description: Arlington, VA : ASCD, [2024] | Includes bibliographical references and index.
Identifiers: LCCN 2024011853 (print) | LCCN 2024011854 (ebook) | ISBN 9781416633037 (paperback) | ISBN 9781416633044 (pdf)
Subjects: LCSH: Motivation in education. | Teacher effectiveness. | Effective teaching. | Teachers—Job stress—Prevention.
Classification: LCC LB1065 .A6332 2024 (print) | LCC LB1065 (ebook) | DDC 371.95/6—dc23/eng/20240416
LC record available at https://lccn.loc.gov/2024011853
LC ebook record available at https://lccn.loc.gov/2024011854

33 32 31 30 29 28 27 26 25 24   1 2 3 4 5 6 7 8 9 10 11 12

To teachers everywhere. You deserve to be fired up and energized professionally, and your students desperately need you to be healthy and happy. Remember, self-care isn't selfish.

REKINDLE YOUR PROFESSIONAL FIRE

1

How We Got Here— and Our Pathway Out

"Self-care is never a selfish act—it is simply good stewardship of the only gift I have, the gift I was put on earth to offer others. Anytime we can listen to [our] true self and give it the care it requires, we do so not only for ourselves but for the many others whose lives we touch."

—Parker Palmer, *Let Your Life Speak: Listening for the Voice of Vocation*

It was my eighth year of teaching when I realized I was burning out.

The first few years of my career were a happy blur. I was passionate about teaching and took a lot of pride in how often parents told me that their children loved coming to school. The hard work and long hours didn't bother me. After all, I knew that teaching was going to be hard work. Both of my parents were teachers. Mom spent Sunday afternoons planning for the week ahead, and I sometimes joined her on afternoons after school and Saturdays in her 3rd grade classroom, cutting out block letters for bulletin boards or helping clean the room. Dad was a professor of music at Bates College, and I spent many an afternoon as a young kid playing in empty classrooms while he finished office work, met with students, and slogged through department meetings. He spent hours on weekends and evenings grading papers, especially as semesters closed down. I remember biking in circles around the college chapel as he rehearsed for upcoming organ recitals and choir concerts.

So I threw myself into the work of being a 4th grade teacher, taking pride in staying at school late into the evenings. I made sure to get the access code to the school security system so that I could enter the building on the weekends to plan and clean my room. There was always so much to do.

Back then, at least in my school, teachers had a ton—maybe even too much—freedom. But I loved it. There were math books stacked in the back of the room, but no one in my school really used the program because it was so dry and dated. So I created my own units, lessons, and materials. We also had science texts that were pretty low level and boring, so I created units of study based on the chapters of the text I wasn't using. We had no real schoolwide approach to literacy instruction, which gave me free rein to try everything I'd learned in college. I set up a reading and writing workshop where students had power and control over what they read and wrote. There was incredible freedom, but that also meant a ton of planning: crafting a scope and sequence, inventing lessons, and creating and collecting materials. Couple this with the two part-time swim coaching jobs I took on, and I worked a lot.

Most days I'd get to school two hours before students arrived to get set for the day. After school, I'd hustle to the pool to coach into the evening. Then, I'd head back to school for another couple of hours before finally heading back to my apartment to crash for the night. Most weekends were split between swim meets and planning, organizing, and cleaning sessions at school.

It was exhausting, but it was also exhilarating. My students and I dove into independent research projects, and I figured out how to facilitate them through trial and error. We adopted a pet snake (a ball python that a precocious student named "Monty"—thanks, Justin). We constructed tissue paper hot air balloons and launched them on the playground. We took mini field trips to local farms and businesses for social studies. Students read books of their choice, and we wrote and self-published tons of stories. I loved teaching—in all of its messy, frustrating, and rewarding glory.

I didn't even really mind the exhaustion, at least not at first. But I also assumed that as I got further into my career, things would ease up. I'd be able to reuse units I'd previously created. I'd have systems in place that would help me feel more settled. I'd have more time on weekends to rest, relax, and exercise. Teaching would still be challenging, but it wouldn't be quite so overwhelming.

There were some other reasons I was so tired—connected with, but not totally caused by—my intense work hours.

For one thing, I wasn't eating very well. I struggled to force myself to go grocery shopping, so I ate way too much junk food. There were four fast-food chains in the 10-minute drive from where I lived to my school, and it was way too easy to stop for meals before and after school. For lunch, I often ate peanut butter and jelly sandwiches on white bread from the school cafeteria and washed them down with chocolate milk.

I also wasn't exercising. Swimming had been my sport from elementary school through college, but by the time I graduated my shoulders were toast, so swimming was out for a while. I was so busy that I didn't carve out time for other forms of exercise.

I wasn't sleeping well, either. Filling up on empty carbs, not exercising, and having a stressful job was taking a toll. When I was in my mid-20s, I was developing joint pain and stiffness, losing muscle mass, and gaining unhealthy weight.

Amid all of this, I got married and started a family. I thought I was tired before? Ha! Our son was almost 2 when our daughter was born. With two little ones at home, I couldn't and didn't want to spend whole Saturdays puttering in my classroom cleaning, organizing, and planning. At the same time, it was harder to get any schoolwork done at home. As sleep deprivation (which has been used as a form of torture, we should recognize) piled up, I struggled to keep up with daily planning and assessing. I had always thought that being a father would make me a better teacher and that being a teacher would make me a better father. Now these two roles were in direct conflict with each other.

I was running myself into the ground. I took on new roles and responsibilities at school: PTA co-president, social studies revision team member, and cooperating teacher were a few. I also took on new roles outside school. Summers were busy with master's degree coursework. Then I began some consulting work for a nonprofit organization, which was an incredible opportunity for growth and a chance to supplement my income to help support our family.

My fire for teaching was starting to sputter. More often than I care to admit, I found myself relying on past lessons and activities that were "good enough." Stacks of daily work piled up on a shelf, only to be frantically gone through in furious catch-up sessions. By the time assessed work got back to students, too much time had passed for it to be terribly valuable. My patience waned and my temper shortened, which was especially tough for my students who needed me at my best.

This was what rankled me the most. As I became more fatigued, both physically and emotionally, it was my students who paid the price. They needed me to be energized and enthusiastic, and that was becoming increasingly more difficult.

With the benefit of hindsight, I can also recognize some other factors were contributing to my sense of burnout that I wasn't fully aware of at the time. Changes were happening in the profession that were having negative impacts on my passion for teaching. The pressures of testing were growing. I didn't really care about standardized test scores, and I resented the time they took away from real teaching and learning. Our district adopted a prescriptive math program to try to address concerns raised by these test scores. Although I was initially relieved to have my planning burden lightened, I lost my zest for teaching math as I blindly followed the program. Too often, I'd glance at the next math lesson a few minutes before teaching it instead of taking the time to adjust lessons or make them better.

Another factor that was reducing my joy of teaching was my lack of connection with colleagues. When Heather and I got married, we moved to New Hampshire and landed together in a new school. At my previous school in Connecticut, there was a sense of camaraderie and excitement about teaching that was infectious. So many of us loved what we did and were excited to share with each other. I developed many strong friendships that made going to school fun. That wasn't the case in my new school. I absolutely loved the students and families with whom I worked, but I wasn't a good fit with many of my colleagues.

It was rough.

How We Got Here

As it turns out, my experience isn't unique. There were many things going on for me at the time that were shared with the broader teaching community.

My teaching career began in the beginning of the push toward standards and the unfortunate resulting move toward standardization. Well-meaning (I'd like to believe) policymakers implemented initiatives such as No Child Left Behind and Race to the Top. Based on the apparent belief that teachers and schools needed to be better motivated to excel, they imposed carrot-and-stick programs narrowly focused on high-stakes standardized tests. Unfortunately, because it's impossible to assess high-level learning (e.g., creative thinking, collaborative learning, leadership, self-motivation, perseverance, and complex problem solving) through bubble-in, short-answer, and formulaic writing tests, these assessments instead focused on low-level, rote skills that were easy to assess (e.g., basic reading comprehension, grammar, and computation).

Not surprisingly, this had the effect of sharpening schools' focus on low-level learning at the expense of higher-level tasks. I remember in the late '90s while teaching in Connecticut, being told by my principal (through clenched teeth against her wishes, I might add) to drop everything else we were doing in writing for six weeks to have kids practice writing five-paragraph essays. What was even worse is that we were supposed to especially focus on helping students who had scored a 6 or 7 on their previous writing test—the "bubble kids." Because an 8 was considered the score showing competence and would be emphasized in reporting in newspapers, students who were on the bubble, or almost competent, were viewed as the key to improving our school's scores. We weren't asked to focus on students who already scored an 8 or higher. Improvement in their scores wouldn't show up anyway. Students who scored a 5 or lower were too far from competent to likely score the coveted 8.

And I was lucky. I was teaching in a suburban school district that had decent enough basic test scores to shield us from the most intense and ridiculous consequences of not making "adequate yearly progress." The effects were, not surprisingly, felt most sharply in poorer communities. Some schools were shut down and taken over by government commissions. Instead of supporting local struggling schools, governments created voucher and school choice programs encouraging families to leave neighborhood schools. More and more federal and state money flowed into private schools and alternative programs, leaving less for already underfunded public ones.

Panicked by the prospect of not "achieving" on these low-level tests, school districts flocked in droves to purchase programs and curricula designed by companies to raise test scores. If you're going to get better at something, you have to practice. So what do these programs often emphasize? You guessed it: low-level and rote work. And in an effort to accelerate learning, this low-level rote work was pushed down into lower and lower grades. Fourth and 5th grades were once the time to practice multiplication facts; now it's 3rd. Walk into a 1st grade classroom today, and it likely looks like a traditional 3rd grade classroom of 30 years ago. Desks are more likely to be in rows. If there are blocks or other building materials, they're not out and available, and good luck finding art supplies out for daily use.

In my own teaching, I felt the repercussions, even beyond the five-paragraph writing emphasis. In the prescriptive math program our district adopted, each unit was laid out in sequential order, and each lesson was spelled out in great detail—requiring all teachers to use the same process, same materials, same practice problems, and same assessments, regardless of whether these were a good match for our students' learning needs. Special education and remedial support times became more rigid, often forcing me to schedule academics at times not conducive to learning (e.g., writing at the end of the day).

You may have seen other changes brought about by an overemphasis on the testing of rote skills—changes that are often mandated and forced on teachers. Some elementary schools have adopted mini high school models where teachers departmentalize and children as young as 1st grade trade classes and teachers for various subjects. Teachers may become more skilled in teaching specific content areas, but this often happens at the expense of child-based teaching, flexible scheduling, and curricular integration. Some teachers are required to post schedules outside classroom doors so that administrators can make sure everyone is on pace and in lockstep with everyone else, again, reducing teachers' ability to flex teaching depending on the needs and flow of a particular group.

Pressures at the secondary level have increased as well. Many middle and high school teachers have shared their frustrations with me about the amount of time they spend communicating with kids and families about points and grades instead of learning. The intensity of the college admissions process seems to have worsened, and for many students, that means it's hard to enjoy the moment as everyone is directing them to think about (and stress out about) the future.

In many places, the frequency and intensity of student disruptions have also increased. We shouldn't be surprised. This can, at least in part, be attributed to many of these changes we've seen in education. We're pushing inappropriately difficult, boring, and low-level content into younger and younger grades. Kids get less downtime. The work isn't as joyful. It's pressure packed. It's a recipe for having kids shut down or rebel.

The loss of teacher autonomy is just one of several factors that has made it harder to fully enjoy our profession. There's no doubt that the number of initiatives schools are taking on has increased in a desperate effort to increase achievement. Taking on too many initiatives leads to everyone feeling incompetent on multiple fronts at once. The past decade has been one of almost nonstop societal dysregulation in the United States, and it shouldn't be surprising that children mirror the culture in which they live. It's been especially challenging as educators, who pour their hearts and souls into their work, have become lightning rods in the culture wars with battles around masking, book bans, equity, gender inclusivity, and other social issues.

This isn't what we signed up for.

Becoming a More Well-Balanced Teacher

But it also doesn't need to drive us from the profession. When I recognized my fire was dwindling, I decided that I either needed to figure out how to better balance my life and reenergize my teaching or needed to start thinking about a new profession. There was no way I was going to spend the next 30 years becoming more and more dour, grumping about "kids these days," and counting down the days to retirement. So I embarked on a personal learning journey to figure out strategies for staying personally and professionally healthy and vibrant.

I started by asking colleagues, both ones in my school as well as ones from around the United States who I met through consulting work, *How do you stay healthy and balanced? How do you juggle family and career?*

(No one had it figured out, by the way. Everyone was just as maxed out as I was.) I read lots of articles and books about health and balance, looking for strategies and ideas that would help. I also engaged in self-reflection and tried to answer some of my burning questions. What parts of my teaching were most important, and what could I let go of? How could I (or even just *could I*) hang on to my passion for teaching while still enjoying my family?

I journaled to process my thinking and collect ideas I was learning. Before long, these journal entries were the beginnings of a book that would eventually become *The Well-Balanced Teacher: How to Work Smarter and Stay Sane Inside the Classroom and Out*.

The irony wasn't lost on me that while struggling with professional burnout and exhaustion from parenting two young children, I was getting up at 4:00 a.m. to work on a book about work-life balance. Yet it fed my need for purpose and professional engagement. Everywhere I looked, teachers were struggling with the same things I was. And as I dug into the work of finding a healthier balance in my life, I stumbled on some things that really worked. I let go of some things that were weighing me down. I carved out time for exercise and found ways to eat healthy foods that fit into a busy teaching schedule. Most important, I rediscovered my teaching mojo. I rekindled my professional fire.

The Well-Balanced Teacher was released in 2010. Now, well over a decade later, the topics and themes explored in that book are more relevant and important than ever. I have also learned so much more. Teachers have shared stories about their own struggles, journeys, and strategies. New research has led to new understandings of how to maintain balance, motivation, and professional engagement.

An especially important new insight came from another project: supporting teachers with student motivation. In my book *Tackling the Motivation Crisis* (2021), I outline six key intrinsic motivators—autonomy, belonging, competence, purpose, curiosity, and fun—that students need to be self-motivated about schoolwork. As I've worked with thousands of teachers across the United States and beyond, quite a few educators have observed, "It's not just kids who need those things. We do, too!" And of course, they're spot-on. These intrinsic motivators serve as the framework for a large portion of this new book.

Our Pathway Out

We all have different challenges when it comes to personal and professional balance, but as it turns out, nearly all fall into one of four categories based on fundamental needs we all have as humans. When these needs are being met, we can be personally balanced and professionally engaged. When they're in deficit, we start to burn out. While one person might be struggling with a loss of curricular autonomy, someone else might need some support with healthy eating and hydration habits. It might be that you're hoping to gain some ideas for how to regain a sense of joy and fun in teaching while your colleague down the hall might need some support with boosting their sense of competence.

In Chapter 2, Recharge Your Battery, you'll focus on our most **basic needs**: healthy eating, hydration, sleep, safety, exercise, and rest and relaxation. You'll learn important ideas about how to shift some personal habits to increase your energy, boost your mood, and reduce your chances of getting sick.

Chapter 3, Recover Your Swagger, explores two important psychological needs: **competence** and **purpose**. This chapter is about confidence. Have you been hanging your head lately and feeling like you're just not doing enough? Are you suffering from initiativitis? Are you struggling with your sense of *why* in teaching? If so, you'll likely find some ideas here that will help.

Chapter 4, Rekindle Your Professional Fire, is about passion. Is your excitement for teaching dwindling? Has your **curiosity** for professional learning and growth been fading? Could it be that you feel like your hands are tied and that you don't have much control over what or how you teach? Without **autonomy** it's almost impossible to be self-motivated. Learn (or remember) how to flex your creative muscles and regain some control—even if you're required to use overly prescriptive programs.

Chapter 5, Refresh Your Spirit, tackles two more key intrinsic motivators: **belonging** and **fun.** In the midst of all of the angst and pressure of our current education climate, we can lose sight of an important truth: teaching and learning should be joyful! What if you could head to school each morning with a spring in your step because you are eager to spend time with your students and colleagues? That's what this chapter is all about.

As you read these chapters, see if you can find one idea that really seems important and worth working on. One of the keys to effective change is to keep goals small and only work on one thing at a time. It could be easy to read this whole book, think of a bunch of areas you'd like to work on, and then get more stressed out as you're overwhelmed by the possibilities. Instead, I suggest that you jot down lots of notes as you read and then find one that feels like a good place to start.

Once you have an area you'd like to work on, check out Chapter 6, How to Build Powerful New Habits. You'll learn about a process and explore practical strategies to help you make changes that actually stick. By the end of the chapter, you'll have everything you need to get going on your journey toward recharging your battery, recovering your swagger, rekindling your professional fire, and refreshing your spirit.

Before you move on to exploring categories and making a plan, there are a few important mindsets to consider that may help you on this journey.

Mindset #1: Self-Care Isn't Selfish (It's the #1 Rule of Lifeguarding)

When I was a teenager, I took the certification course to be a lifeguard. One lesson came as a bit of a shock. We were learning how to perform open-water rescues. These are incidents where a victim is struggling in deep water, such as a lake or the ocean. If the victim is panicked, we were taught to swim to within a few body lengths of the person and try and get them to calm down. "Hi. I'm Mike, and I'm here to help. Try to calm your body down, and I'll give you a hand." If the victim doesn't calm down—here was the shocking part for me—we were told to stay a few body lengths away and wait until they were unconscious. Then we were to grab them, bring them in to shore, and perform CPR to try and save them. I couldn't believe this. We were supposed to let someone become unconscious?! Weren't we supposed to be the hero and swim in and rescue them? But our instructor explained that no matter how strong you are, if you get tangled up with someone hopped up on adrenaline, chances are that you now have two people drowning, not one. And if you're drowning, you're not able to help the person you're there to save. *In order to have a chance at helping someone else, you have to take care of yourself first.*

A barrier to good self-care goal setting can be (often subconscious) guilt. Educators are care*givers*. We spend incredible time and energy taking care of others. This is one of our superpowers, but it can also be our Kryptonite. When our sense of purpose is derived from taking care of others, self-care can feel selfish. We have our students at school and families at home who need our time and energy. How can we possibly make time to take care of ourselves with meetings to attend, assignments to assess, emails to read and write, and our own families to care for?

If this is getting in your way, here's a workaround to try: Frame self-care as part of caring for others. Your students need you to be healthy and balanced. It's almost impossible to be patient with a student who is struggling if you are exhausted, overwhelmed, or cranky. Your family and friends benefit when you're centered and in good spirits. You need to engage in self-care to be healthy and balanced.

When viewed through the first rule of lifeguarding, self-care is no longer selfish. Others need you to take care of yourself, so it's no longer selfish to exercise or spend time on projects that give you good energy.

Mindset #2: Don't Wait to Be Rescued

No doubt, it would be fantastic if school and district leaders played an active role in supporting faculty engagement. In fact, I can't imagine why this wouldn't be one of their top priorities. I'm sure they want it to be. At the end of each of Chapters 2–5, you'll find suggestions for "taking it schoolwide." These are strategies that teachers and school leaders can work on together to support cultures of positive engagement.

School leaders need to go beyond telling teachers to "make sure to take care of yourselves" after they've just spent 45 minutes telling them about all of the new initiatives they'll be taking on. It's also important to recognize that leaders are just as overwhelmed and exhausted as teachers, sometimes even more so. If you wait for administration to come to the rescue, you might be waiting a long, long time. Additionally, teachers have such diverse strengths, questions, and struggles that I'm not sure how administration could possibly come up with a way to differentiate support for all our varying needs. You, as an individual, will likely have a better shot of figuring out what you need to rekindle your professional fire than someone else will. This is something we should all work on together.

Mindset #3: Want to Improve? That Means Something Needs to Change

Pete Hall is a former classroom teacher and principal who now supports teachers around the world with great teaching and personal and professional engagement. Pete was once giving a keynote address to a large group of teachers at a beginning-of-the-year kick-off event. His high energy was infectious, and teachers were getting fired up. He was talking about professional engagement and learning and growing as educators. "So how many of you want to improve your practice and get better at teaching this year?" he asked. Hands flew up all over the auditorium. "Great! So how many of you want to change?" he continued. There was a startled pause by the group as people nervously chuckled and looked around uncomfortably. A few hands went up tentatively. Pete smiled and winked playfully at the group. "Y'all know that change is a prerequisite to growth."

This is such an important idea. It's easy to say we want to improve, to learn, to grow. It's harder to say we want to change. But how can we possibly grow, learn, or improve without changing anything?

Mindset #4: It's All About Habits— Getting Stuck in the Right Ruts

Have you ever hopped in the car on a Saturday morning to drive to the store and instead found yourself accidentally driving to school? You got into the car and autopilot kicked in. You're so used to driving to school that it happens automatically if you're not careful.

What are some other habits you have? What routines are so ingrained in your day that they happen automatically? Chances are that you have some healthy ones. Do you brush your teeth after breakfast? Walk the dog before dinner? Call your parents every Sunday evening? Chances are equally good that you have some unhealthy ones. Maybe you sip soda throughout the day, watch TV too late in the evening, or doomscroll news sites on your phone when you have downtime.

There's good news and bad news about habits. The bad news is that once you're in an unhealthy habit, it's hard to change. The good news is that once you're in a healthy habit, it's easy to keep it going.

I remember as a young teacher worrying about getting stuck in ruts as I got older. Now that I am older, I have come to realize that we all get stuck in ruts. The key to health and balance is to get stuck in the *right* ruts. So let's dig into this in some more depth. How do habits form, and how can focusing on routines help lead us to real change?

How Do Habits Form?

In his book *The Power of Habit*, Charles Duhigg (2013) explains how habits form. There is a three-step habit loop: cue, routine, reward. The cue is a trigger that initiates the loop. The routine is the action you take as a result of the cue. The reward is the result of the routine that encourages your brain to repeat this loop. This loop explains how both healthy and unhealthy habits form and solidify.

For example, one morning you happen to wake up earlier than normal. You get up and head into school 30 minutes ahead of schedule. Not only do you hit less traffic, but you get way more work done because there are fewer colleagues to talk to earlier in the morning. Your plans are more solid, you have a much better day, and you feel a glow of success. You think that it's worth repeating. So that night, you hit the hay a bit early and set your alarm 30 minutes earlier than your previous wake-up time. Once again, your day goes better with an early start. The cue was the early wake up. The routine was heading to school early. The reward was the glow of success. If you keep repeating this loop, eventually, you'll find yourself in a better morning habit.

Here's an example of a negative habit. It's midafternoon, students have left for the day, and you're exhausted. You had a particularly rough interaction with a student. A colleague pops in to ask how your day went. You share about how that one student ruined a whole lesson and how often they drive you crazy. Your colleague empathizes and to help you feel better shares a similar frustration. It feels good to let it all out and to have someone who really understands. Misery loves company, and you actually feel a real sense of belonging with your colleague. The next day, the same colleague stops by, and you immediately fall back into talking about a rough student interaction. It feels so good to vent! Before you know it, this turns into a routine. The cue is frustration. The routine is grumping about students. The reward is the sense of belonging. The problem is that complaining never gets you closer to a solution, and you're actually reliving the trauma of the rough day—bathing your brain in more stress chemicals, and making success tomorrow just a little bit harder.

How Do You Focus on Changing Routines?

Duhigg (2013) explains that it's really hard to extinguish a bad habit. Cues and rewards are especially sticky. Instead, he suggests focusing on the specific part of the habit loop that's easier to change—the routine (p. 62). Let's explore how this might work with our previous example. Let's say that you've recognized the negative habit you're in. It's not really helping, and you don't want to always complain about your students. Chances are that the cue is going to stick around—you're always going to have challenging students, and you'll be tired at the end of each day. So how might you shift the routine? Try thinking ahead: What's a small success or something positive you could share at the end of the day? You can still connect and feel a sense of belonging with your colleague, but you can reinforce your sense of competence instead of cycling around negative events with students and feeling incompetent (and then guilty for speaking badly about kids).

In the final chapter of this book, you'll learn a simple three-step process for how to put all of this into action: how to shift routines and habits so that you can be successful with your new goal.

Let's Dig In. What Are Your Rocks?

Have you heard the famous analogy of the rocks, pebbles, and sand? I first heard this story years ago, told by a dear and wise colleague.

In this story, a professor of philosophy is standing before his class. He had a large empty glass jar. His class watches as he pulls a bag of rocks out from under the table. He pours the rocks into the jar until the rocks come all the way to the top.

He asks his students, "Is the jar full?"

They respond that it is, nodding with confidence. They can see the rocks filled all the way to the top of the jar.

He then pulls out a bag of pebbles and pours them into the jar. The pebbles trickle down through the rocks, filling in gaps. The professor keeps pouring until no more pebbles can fit. Students chuckle, recognizing their mistake.

He asks his students again, "Is the jar full?"

Again, they nod and say that it is. It's clear that no more pebbles will fit in the jar.

Once again, the professor reaches under the table. This time he pulls out a bag of sand. He pours the sand into the jar, and the sand seeps down between the rocks and pebbles, filling the empty spaces.

The professor then says to his class, "The jar is your life, and you must consider how you fill it. The rocks are what are most important—your family and friends, your physical and emotional health, and a fulfilling career. Everything else is pebbles and sand."

He continued, "The key to a satisfying life is to make sure to fill your jar correctly. If you begin with sand and pebbles, you won't have space for the rocks."

As you explore the next chapters, look for some rocks. By Chapter 6, be ready to tackle one, and you'll learn how to make a plan to get going.

Are you ready to begin your journey? Let's go!

2

Recharge Your Battery

Count Rugen: Are you coming down into the pit? Wesley's got his strength back. I'm starting him on the machine tonight.

Prince Humperdinck: Tyrone, you know how much I love watching you work, but I've got my country's 500th anniversary to plan, my wedding to arrange, my wife to murder, and Guilder to frame for it. I'm swamped.

Count Rugen: Get some rest. If you haven't got your health, you haven't got anything.

—*The Princess Bride*

It's not news to any of us that healthy foods, good exercise, and good sleep are foundational to our health. Yet creating and maintaining healthy habits can feel so hard to do amid a challenging career. If you're a parent or caregiver outside school, it is that much harder.

Although most of this book is about boosting professional energy and engagement, we know from Abraham Maslow that without some key healthy foundations, it will be hard to move on to loftier goals. Just as teachers often say "Maslow before Bloom" to remind themselves to take care of students' basic needs in order to support higher-level learning, so too should we keep this idea in mind. Perhaps we should all start wearing WWMD ("What Would Maslow Do?") bracelets as a reminder.

Without taking care of our most basic needs, it's going to be hard to have the positive energy that students desperately need for us to have. So let's explore a few key ideas about how we can make sure our batteries are well charged.

Eat Well

Michael Pollan is a journalist who has researched and written extensively about food and the food industry in the United States. In his book *In Defense of Food* (2009), he offers a simple set of guidelines for healthful eating: eat food, not too much, mostly plants. It sounds so easy, doesn't it?

Yet it's so easy to eat poorly. Remember how I got into bad eating habits early in my career? At one point I was hiding McDonald's wrappers under other trash in my classroom's trash can so that my students wouldn't know what I was eating for breakfast. (I was teaching a nutrition unit in science and didn't want to set a bad example.)

All of that junk I ate—breakfast sandwiches, hash browns, burgers, fries, white bread, and peanut butter with sugar added—doesn't qualify as "real food" according to Michael Pollan. It was all highly processed and loaded with unhealthy preservatives, unnatural fats, and sugars. It's perhaps not surprising that I was 35 pounds heavier than I am now and was starting to suffer from knee and lower back pain as well as digestive issues. I was starting to feel like an old man about three years after I had to start shaving on a regular basis.

I hope you haven't fallen quite as far as I had, but I bet you've got an unhealthy food habit or two that could use reshaping. Perhaps you sip soda, energy drinks, or iced coffee (made and sweetened by someone else) throughout the day. It might be that you have a stash of candy in your room that you peck away at in the afternoon. Maybe you skip breakfast all together, unable to muster the energy to eat before school, or perhaps you eat a pastry or donut, full of sugar and devoid of the protein or vitamins and minerals you need to have good energy throughout the day.

As you consider some potential habits to change, remember to keep your goals simple and reasonable. Asking me to prepare seven sets of meals a week when I was 23 and overwhelmed wouldn't have helped at all. However, I could have made my own tea at home and kept bananas and natural peanut butter in my classroom for breakfast (both habits I eventually adopted).

Also keep this idea in mind. If you're a parent, by shifting a few habits to be healthier for yourself, you can shift these same habits for your children, letting them reap the benefits of your healthier habits.

Here are a few other healthy eating habits to consider.

Cook Large Meals

Make a large meal on Sunday and pack leftovers for several lunches during the week. Foods you prepare yourself will almost always be healthier than foods you grab on the go. You can control which ingredients are and aren't included, and it won't be full of chemical preservatives. After your big meal, pack lunch-size portions for your first few lunches of the week. As a bonus, you'll almost certainly save money and generate less packaging waste in the process.

Use Healthy Prepared Foods and Avoid Heavily Processed Ones

If you're looking to keep meal prep short, consider prepackaged foods that are healthy. Although many prepackaged foods are loaded with preservatives, salt, and sugar, there are some that are packed with good nutrition. Matthew Kadey (2023), a registered dietician and nutrition writer, offers five examples of foods that fit the bill: premade salad mixes (especially ones with dark leafy greens), precooked frozen shrimp, canned beans, hummus, and frozen waffles made with whole grains. Look for prepared meals that include real foods (beans, wheat, fruits, vegetables, etc.), and avoid ones with ingredients on their labels you can't pronounce.

Eat Healthy Protein for Breakfast

Protein in the morning is so important. It gives long-term energy, helps regulate your appetite throughout the day, keeps your blood sugar stable, and offers many other health benefits. Bananas with peanut butter, flavored cottage cheese, hard-boiled eggs, Greek yogurt mixed with granola, and oatmeal with nuts are all nutrient-dense foods that are easy to prepare and even store on a shelf or in a mini fridge at school. Your students will appreciate your more stable mood, and your focus and attention will be sharper as you teach lessons and confer with students.

Keep Healthy Snacks on Hand

You're going to get hungry at some point during the day, and you're likely to grab what's nearby. If you've got a drawer full of candy and chips, guess what you're going to eat? Instead, make sure those easy on-hand foods are good for you. There are plenty of healthier options that can sit on a shelf and are easy to grab: a bag of almonds, a big box of raisins or other dried fruit (dates, craisins, and apricots are some of my favorites), and a bunch of bananas are all great options.

Stay Hydrated

"My schedule is so packed I don't even have time to pee!" is the lament of many a teacher. So what do you do? You intentionally dehydrate yourself so that you won't need to use the bathroom during a two-hour block in your schedule when you can't leave your room. And how does this work out? By the end of the morning, you have a dull headache building, it's hard to focus on reading conferences with your students, and you're getting cranky.

On the upside, your bladder isn't screaming at you. Many teachers have told me that their doctors relayed to them that teachers seemed to have high rates of urinary tract and bladder infections because they can't use the restroom when they need to. Here are a few hydration ideas to consider.

Find a Bathroom Buddy

Is there a teacher nearby who can watch your class for a couple of minutes so that you can use the bathroom? Perhaps they'd like to trade favors. You can pop into their room each day at 10:00, and they can give you a quick break at 11:00. One year, my next-door colleague and I had a standing agreement. If either of us needed a quick break, we could pop our head in next door and check in with a quick thumbs-up. If we got one in return, we knew we could run down the hall for a minute.

Sip Healthy Drinks

Another hydration challenge to look out for doesn't involve *when* to hydrate but *how*. If you can use the restroom at humane intervals, you might be able to sip liquids throughout the day. If so, make sure you're sipping something healthy. Although drinking soda, sports drinks, juice cocktails, and iced coffees from your local café might be fine every now and then, sipping sugar and chemicals all day every day can pile up negatively in the long run. Instead, go for water. If you use a reusable water bottle, you'll save a boatload of money and send a whole lot less plastic to your local landfill. Or if you want to spruce things up, try flavored seltzer. It's got the feel of soda without the sugar.

Start Each Day with a Glass of Water

This is one of the simplest ways to boost hydration. Before you start brewing your coffee. Before you take the dog out. Before you do anything else. Drink a tall glass of water. This helps flush toxins in your body, improves digestion, and helps you start the day with proper hydration.

Sleep Well

According to renowned sleep expert Matthew Walker, sleep is the great elixir of life. Sleep has all kinds of impressive benefits. It helps us consolidate and integrate daily learning, lowers our blood pressure and heart rate, boosts our immune system functions, aids in emotional recovery, and boosts our creative problem-solving abilities (Walker, n.d.). The Centers for Disease Control and Prevention (2022) currently recommends that adults get at least seven hours of sleep a night, which is easier said than done. Here are a few suggestions for improving sleep habits.

Schedule Sleep

We put a meeting on our calendar to make sure we don't miss it. What if we did the same for sleep? First, figure out when you need to get up. Perhaps it's 5:30. Next, determine how much sleep you need to be really rested. Let's say that's eight hours. That means you'd need to be asleep by

9:30. So on your calendar, schedule 9:30–5:30 for sleep. You might also want to carve out 9:00–9:30 for getting ready for bed, so you have time to brush your teeth, get clothes ready for the morning, and read a bit before turning off the light. Having a consistent bedtime is one of the most powerful ways to support good sleep habits.

Pay Attention to the Last Few Hours Before Bedtime

What we do before bedtime has a huge impact on what happens when we lie down. Drinking alcohol before bed might make us more relaxed and may even get us to sleep more quickly, but it diminishes deep sleep and makes us more likely to wake up in the middle of the night. Many phone, computer, tablet, and TV screens throw off light that messes with our circadian rhythm. Turn devices off a while before you go to bed, and don't turn them on in bed, either. The content we consume in the evening may also make us more agitated as well. After realizing how upset I was getting after scrolling through news sites, I've made a personal rule that I won't look at news apps on my phone once I've had dinner. I'm able to relax a good bit more before bedtime now.

Be Aware of Caffeine

Did you know that caffeine has a 10-hour half-life? That means that if you drink a cup of coffee at noon, 50 percent of the caffeine is still circulating in your body at 10:00 p.m. (Walker, n.d.). My sleep improved dramatically when I went from two cups of coffee to one in the morning. I now sip herbal tea instead of the second cup of coffee. If you feel the need of a midday pick-me-up, and you're sensitive to caffeine, you might try a short brisk walk. If you can get outside for the walk, that's even better. Even a lap or two around your school building at lunch can boost your energy and mood and not disrupt your sleep later.

Take Care of Your Safety

During my wife's second year as a 2nd grade teacher, she had a student in her classroom who was at the center of an international kidnapping scandal. His mother had whisked him out of their home country after she found out that her husband (who was the equivalent of semi-royalty) had been abusing him. My wife had to keep her classroom door locked at all times but couldn't tell her students why, of course. She had very specific instructions for what to do if men came to capture her student (back off and let them). She had to carry instructions for what police number to call and what coded message to relay if anything happened. Fortunately, none of this came to pass, but after students left after the last day of school in June, she broke down sobbing. She hadn't fully realized how scared and anxious she was until it was over.

It's heartbreaking that this category even needs to be included in this book. We shouldn't have to worry about basic safety in our line of work. But, of course, we do. There's no need to go into this in great depth here because we all see news stories about school shootings and other horrible events. Chances are you've had incidents in your school where teachers have been hit, kicked, bitten, or worse by students. There have been threats against teachers and administrators by community members in reaction to perceived slights or differences of opinion.

What can we do? There are no easy answers, but here are a few you might try.

If you're worried about what to do if something scary happens, make sure you know what procedures to follow. You might even practice them. That's what fire drills are for—to make sure we've all rehearsed what to do if a fire breaks out. Though things like active shooter drills might be scary, knowing what we're supposed to do can at least give us a small measure of a sense of control over our anxiety.

You might also consider finding a trusted mentor or administrator with whom to talk. They may have information or advice that can help. At the very least, the act of sharing your concerns may help alleviate some stress.

If you have a student who is being threatening or aggressive, either with other students or with you, get help. Is there a school counselor or resource officer who can give you some support? Is there a union representative who might be able to help? Especially if you have asked for help from administration and feel like you're not getting the support you need, this might be a necessary next step.

Finally, you might need to know when it's time to get out of an unsafe environment. A good friend of mine started his teaching career at a high school in rural Maine. He had a confrontation with one of his students who was on parole in which the student threatened to stab him. When my friend realized that administration wasn't going to support him and have the student removed (the student returned to class the next day with a forced note of apology), he decided to leave the school midyear. It clearly wasn't ideal, but he decided that his own safety needed to take priority.

Again, there are no easy answers here. Perhaps what's most important is to recognize that a sense of safety is one of our most fundamental needs. If you're feeling unsafe, it will be hard to engage in great teaching or to support your students' great learning.

Exercise

We all know how important it is to move our bodies on a regular basis. It can lower our risk for all kinds of health problems later in life: diabetes, heart disease, cancer, and high blood pressure are just a few. Exercise can also help us more immediately. Even short and non-strenuous movement sessions can boost our mood, improve our digestion, reduce stress, and help us get better sleep.

For many of us, building an exercise routine can seem overwhelming. I was recently talking with a relative at a holiday gathering, and he said, "I know I need to start exercising, but I don't even know where to start. I think I need a trainer."

You don't need a trainer. It doesn't have to be that hard or expensive. If you're not exercising at all, even a little is better than what you're not doing now. Start by going for a 10-minute walk several times a week. Bring sneakers to school and walk around the neighborhood right after busses leave. You'll probably find that you'll have better energy for planning after a quick movement break.

If you're already exercising a little but would like to increase it, try adding 5–10 minutes to what you're already doing. If you're walking every day, try walking a bit faster. Start a walking group for colleagues to give yourself company and more motivation to get out there.

You may be worried that you're too old to start exercising, but it's never too late. In an inspirational episode of *Limitless* with Chris Hemsworth, a show about simple ways to boost health and longevity, two seniors are highlighted. One started cycling in his 50s as a way to drop some weight. He nearly collapsed from exhaustion after biking around the block when he first started. Now in his 70s, he's biking hundreds of kilometers a week. Another started weightlifting in her 50s. At 85, she now runs exercise groups for others in her community and looks strong and agile (Aronofsky et al., 2022). I started running in my 40s and have less lower back and knee pain than I did 15 years ago. As a longevity expert in the episode says, "We don't stop moving when we get old. We get old when we stop moving."

Here are a few more ideas to get you going.

Find an Activity That You Enjoy

I think we sometimes get stuck in the mindset that exercise is supposed to be uncomfortable or unpleasant. No doubt, there are some days when I'm running that don't feel so great. But on the whole, it feels good. I love being outside. I love having some music to bop along to as I pound out the miles. The other day a huge deer crossed the road right in front of me, and it was exhilarating.

You may hate running. No problem. Do you like to bike? Swim? Walk? Dance? What's something you enjoy doing that gets you moving? Do that instead. If you can find a form of exercise that's enjoyable, it will be way easier to get yourself to stick with a routine.

Remember That Easy Exercise Is Still Exercise

It's also important to recognize that exercise doesn't need to hurt to be worthwhile. Despite what Gatorade and Nike commercials might have you believe, you don't need to be gasping for breath and bent in half exhausted in order for working out to "count."

In fact, even world-class runners spend a majority of their workout time at an easy effort level. Eliud Kipchoge is arguably the greatest marathoner in the history of the sport. He runs 26.2 miles at a pace faster than most commercial treadmills will go on their highest setting. He is a two-time Olympic gold medalist and has won numerous major marathons multiple times. At age 37, he won the 2022 Berlin marathon, shattering his own world record by 30 seconds (Watta, 2022). A video of Eliud and a few others in his running group shows them heading out for a daily training run where they're going so slowly that they barely look like they're running (Hambleton, 2021). His coach calls this pace the "Kenyan shuffle." Though they'll speed up as they go, most of their running will be at a "conversational pace," or a pace easy enough that you can carry on a conversation without being out of breath. Runners should spend most of their time in this pace to get the benefits of aerobic exercise while minimizing their injury risk.

Even easy exercise is incredibly beneficial. Walking 10 minutes a day is way better than not walking 10 minutes a day, so set an exercise goal that is easy enough that you'll be comfortable and it stays enjoyable.

Find a Group—or Start One

You might enjoy exercising on your own. It's certainly easier to be flexible if you don't have to coordinate with others. However, there's something powerful about having others who you exercise with. When I was a classroom teacher, I had a swimming group that I met with several days a week before school. We took turns bringing in workouts for the group and pushed each other as we swam. It was motivational knowing that a couple of buddies were counting on me being there each day.

Is there a local pickleball league or a disc golf club you could join? Most local groups like this cater to all ages and abilities, even people who are just trying them for the first time. These can be especially helpful if you're looking for some guidance and direction, as there's usually someone who organizes these groups and gives some structure and support.

You could also start your own group. One teacher I worked with early in my career started an after-school walking and running club for students, in part to give her a structured way to get out on the track herself.

Move as You Teach

Dan Buettner has spent decades studying longevity and has shared many of his discoveries in *Live to 100: Secrets of the Blue Zones*. One of these is that in places where people live extraordinarily long and vibrant lives, they engage in lots of natural daily movement. They garden. They walk up steep hills going to church. They do many daily chores by hand.

We might try this at school. As students work, walk around the room to confer and coach instead of calling them to your desk. As you work with them, squat down on their level and rise intentionally with your thighs as you stand. You can park on the far side of the parking lot to get in a few extra steps each morning and afternoon. One high school teacher I spoke with said that he intentionally plans movement-based discussion structures for his students because he moves when they do. A middle school teacher explained that she got rid of her desk in part to force herself to move around the room more. These might seem like small things, but that's kind of the point. Lots of small movements pile up over time.

Exercise with Your Children

If you're a parent, getting into better exercise routines might feel that much tougher, but it doesn't have to be. Is there a way you can exercise with your children? Or can you use their schedules to structure some movement time for yourself?

When our son was an infant, my wife and I were both on a masters swim team. Some days we would trade off swimming and watching our son. He'd sleep blissfully—soothed by the warm moist pool deck air and lulled by the sounds of splashing—while we each got in a half an hour of swimming. When both of our children were young, we would strap them into the double stroller and take vigorous walks, trading off pushing the stroller. (Pushing two small kids in a bulky double stroller up the hill near our house was a serious workout!) Some parents find ways of roping their kids into exercising with them: running at the track, playing basketball, or going for hikes.

If your kids are involved in after-school activities and you're their personal chauffeur, could you exercise while they're taking flute lessons, learning to paint, at soccer practice, or at their Girl Scouts meeting? Is there a track or a park nearby? Could you walk some sets of stairs on nearby bleachers?

Exercise as You Enjoy Digital Content

We spend so much time on our devices. We scroll social media posts on the couch and binge Netflix shows in the evenings. The case could perhaps be made that consuming less of this content might be beneficial, but perhaps you could leverage this time for exercise instead. My father-in-law rides a stationary bike while watching online courses and instructional videos on YouTube. I know many people who listen to podcasts as they walk or run. You could even put down an exercise mat in front of the TV and do some yoga or engage in stretching or light strength training.

Rest and Relax

Technology is a blessing and a curse when it comes to work-life balance. On the one hand, being able to check email, listen to education podcasts, work on lesson plans, and chat with parents on the phone from anywhere is freeing. We can work from home, at the laundromat, at Jiffy Lube, and even while commuting.

On the other hand, we can work from home, at the laundromat, at Jiffy Lube, and even while commuting. Although being able to work from anywhere allows us to potentially be more productive and gives us the flexibility to pick our kids up on time, it can also make it hard to disconnect from work. It feels like we're always on.

Our brains need breaks. We need to learn how to hit the pause button and schedule downtime so that we can really recharge our batteries and have the positive energy to do great work when we're working. The following ideas offer a few places to start. That being said, if you're experiencing significant stress, anxiety, or other mental health issues, make sure to seek the help of a health professional.

Practice Mindfulness and Meditation

Many of us are experiencing more workplace stress than ever before. In many schools (nearly every one I've worked in over the past five years), teachers are reporting more students who are struggling with emotional regulation. So many more kids seem to be on the edge of fight, flight, or freeze. Additionally, many are also seeing more parents who are struggling to make ends meet and are emotionally dysregulated.

You may find yourself burdened with the weight of work. You lie awake at night thinking of students you know are hurting. You have a hard time shaking an angry interaction with a parent, even though you know you didn't do anything wrong. Try practicing mindfulness or a few minutes of meditation. You can learn to redirect thoughts that are doing more harm than good. You can practice breathing and thought techniques that can lower your heart rate and reduce anxiety. This is something you can even practice in the middle of a busy day at school.

You might know Dan Harris as an ABC News journalist. He has been the co-anchor of *Nightline* and weekend editions of *Good Morning America*. He is also a self-described skeptic who eventually found his way to meditation. A workaholic and incessant worrier, Dan suffered secondary trauma after serving as a war correspondent. He ended up self-medicating with drugs and eventually had a panic attack on live television. In his book *10% Happier: How I Tamed the Voice in My Head, Reduced Stress Without Losing My Edge, and Found Self-Help That Actually Helps—A True Story* (2014), he makes the case that even small moments of mindfulness and meditation have significant benefits. He often carves out five minutes in the office to clear his mind and practice mindful breathing.

I've found that when I'm feeling anxious, even just a few slow deep breaths—where I really pay attention to how my breath feels going in and out—help me calm down and reset.

Connect with Nature

It's only been in the last hundred or so years that so many of our species have become almost completely disconnected from the natural world. And it's not good. We reap all kinds of physical and emotional benefits from connecting with nature. A simple walk in nature (as opposed to a walk in an urban setting) can reduce anxiety and increase working memory (Bratman et al., 2015). Various studies have found that nature-based recreation and mental health can improve people's affect and cognition, boost their well-being, and decrease symptoms of anxiety and depression (Lackey et al., 2021). In his bestseller, *Last Child in the Woods*, Ricard Louv (2008) makes the compelling case that our children may be suffering from nature-deficit disorder and that we would all benefit greatly from more time spent outdoors.

Is there a park or perhaps a nature trail through the woods near your school? Can you get outside for 10 minutes in the middle of the day for some fresh air and sunshine? Leave your phone in your classroom and take a couple of laps around your building. Be present. Feel the wind. In the winter, notice the sparkle of sun on ice. It's amazing how just a bit of air and sun can boost your mood. If there are birds singing in the trees, a breeze ruffling leaves, grasshoppers jumping and flying near your feet, or a stream burbling nearby, your spirits can be lifted even more.

Do you have space for a few houseplants in your school space? There is a wide variety available, many of which do well with low light and little care. Still, even the care is soothing. Watering plants can be amazingly calming and therapeutic. The vibe of natural plants in the classroom can be good for students, too. They soften noises and bring a homey natural feel to the classroom. You might also consider setting up a fish tank or installing a bird feeder outside your window. There are tons of small ways to bring a bit of nature into school.

And, of course, try to find time when you're not in school to reconnect with nature as well. Can you take a walk before or after school around your neighborhood? How about a hike on the weekend? Or a bike ride?

Pursue a Hobby

When you're not working on schoolwork, do you have something you like to do? I've been collecting baseball cards since I was about 9. Sorting a few cards and placing them in albums is so satisfying. When the weather is nice, I love to garden. I occasionally take on a house project. I even consider running a hobby, even though it's also exercise. I read running blogs and enjoy searching out possible races to try.

What are some things you love to do that help you rest and relax? If you don't currently have a hobby, is there one you used to enjoy that you could pick back up? Is there something you've always wanted to try, such as painting, scrapbooking, cooking, brewing beer, or photography?

Spend Time with Family and Friends

Many of us found out just how precious together time was during the height of the COVID-19 pandemic. It was heartbreaking to miss holidays with parents and grandparents. It was so hard not to gather with friends for dinner.

And people found really creative ways to get together because the need for connection was so strong. Many played games online with family. We watched movies with friends using screensharing apps. Neighborhoods took turns hosting campfire get-togethers, even in the cold of the winter.

Let's not forget that. Let's cherish our ability to be with others. Make time for family and friends. Carve out weekend time to reconnect with friends. Schedule date nights with your partner to make sure you stay close. Go to your kids' karate tournaments and chess club events.

It's easy, perhaps, to fall into a mindset of personal care as some kind of burden. Chris Hemsworth, an Australian actor perhaps best known for his role as Thor in Marvel movies, has a different perspective. "The prescription is simple. Eat and sleep well. Challenge my mind and body with new experiences and immerse myself in nature—away from the distractions and stress of modern life. And crucially—share all of this with the people I love. None of these simple acts are bitter medicine. They're things I love to do anyway—things I want to do more often" (Aronofsky et al., 2022).

Taking It Schoolwide

In addition to paying attention to supporting our individual needs for hydration, healthy foods, exercise, sleep, and downtime, we might also consider ideas for supporting these needs with our colleagues. How can we nurture healthy habits across the whole school? Here are a few ideas to consider.

Create a Buddy/Trio System for Safety

In some schools that are in neighborhoods prone to violence, teachers are buddied up so that everyone has a go-to person when they need to head to their cars after school, especially if people are leaving as it's getting dark. Could you try a system like this in your school? You might put colleagues in groups of two or three according to where they're located in the school. If someone is feeling threatened by a student or needs immediate help with a scary situation, they can call on one of their buddies.

Consider If You Can Eat Healthy Food in the Cafeteria

In too many schools, food offered to students isn't very healthy. Tater tots, pizza, and canned corn might technically meet FDA requirements of some kind or other, but they're full of sodium and empty carbs. Wouldn't everyone—students and faculty—benefit from unprocessed whole foods that taste good and give real nourishment? Perhaps your school could take this on as a project. You might meet with your food services director to share ideas or write a grant to get more healthy food into the school. Not only would this make meal prep easier (no need to pack a lunch if there's a good one waiting in the cafeteria), but teachers and students would have better moods and attention all afternoon.

Take Care of One Another with Healthy Foods at Staff Gatherings

One way we take care of each other is with food. We might take turns bringing in snacks for faculty or PLC meetings. We might have occasional staff breakfasts or lunches put on by the PTA or a school's sunshine committee. I have often been at schools where teachers brought in snacks or foods for a potluck-style lunch on a professional development day. And so often, the foods we bring in to share are unhealthy. I remember one instance in particular during a summer workshop. There were a few healthy snacks on the table: cherry tomatoes, bananas, dried apricots, and almonds. However, most of the food was ultra-processed and low in nutrients: buttered popcorn, pork rinds, doughnuts, gummy bears, cheddar-flavored potato chips, corn chips, marshmallow peanuts, and cookies. Why do we do that to ourselves and one another? What if we committed to only bringing in healthy foods and drinks for these gatherings?

You might provide a list of recommended foods for events (e.g., hard-boiled eggs, whole grain breads, yogurt, peanut butter, fresh fruit, coffee, tea, orange juice for breakfast) and even a list of foods to avoid bringing in (e.g., donuts, muffins, pastries, sugar-coated cereals, fruit juice cocktails, soda). People can, of course, still bring in unhealthy foods if that's what they want to eat themselves, but what if foods to be shared with others were only healthy ones? Might that be an even better form of taking care of one another through food?

Pay Attention to Schoolwide Healthy Hydration

Many schools now have hydration stations—places to fill your water bottle—right near bathrooms and water fountains. If yours doesn't, this might be something to look into. Could it be built into next year's budget? Is there a grant you might write to bring healthy drinking water so that it's available for all students and adults in your school?

On the other hand, perhaps as a faculty you could make sure there were no unhealthy hydration options in your school. Could you get rid of soda machines or make sure they only stock seltzers? Again, just like with foods, this doesn't mean not allowing teachers to bring soda to school if they want—it just means that only healthy options are offered and easily accessible for all.

Commit to Honoring Downtime

Some schools develop cultures of workaholism. Teachers send emails to families on weekends. Administrators send emails to faculty at midnight. Kids are assigned schoolwork on weekends and holidays. These habits all send the message that we're always on—always working. What if your school were to have a discussion about making certain downtimes sacred? You might agree that weekends are for rest and relaxation, so kids shouldn't be assigned homework, and teachers shouldn't send emails.

Some schools are even carving out a quiet space in schools for teachers. Imagine having a room in your school where you could go when you need to engage in a few minutes of mindful breathing or quiet relaxation. You knew if you went there, others wouldn't talk with you. The lights would be low, there would be some comfortable places to sit, and you could reset. Wouldn't that be an amazing space and a gift for all staff?

Take on a Schoolwide Project to Connect with Nature

There are so many great ways schools are already helping get students and faculty outside to connect with nature. The middle school that my two children went to had an outdoor classroom. It had a set of terraced benches set into the side of a hill with a crushed stone base where a teacher could stand facing students. The simple space was put together by a few teachers who wrote a grant one year.

If you don't already have one, could you put in a garden? You might create a butterfly garden to attract beneficial insects and birds—a space to connect with classrooms' work around insect life cycles, ecosystems, plants, or any number of other science topics. Or you might create a vegetable garden. Students can plant seeds and nurture young plants in the spring, families can volunteer to water and weed throughout the summer, and you can celebrate with a feast in the fall.

If you don't have an area that seems suitable for a full garden, you could build simple wooden boxes to plant or get creative in. Ron Finley is known as the Gangsta Gardener and has become famous for helping transform urban areas into oases of beauty and food production. He has all kinds of incredible ideas for transforming "junk" into planters: dresser drawers, teapots, and even old luggage. (You can learn more about Ron and his work and find a link to his MasterClass at ronfinley.com.)

There are so many other ideas. Create an indoor space near bright windows for houseplants and an indoor fountain. Make walking paths through the woods or prairie behind the school. Put in a small pond. Install a large fish tank near the front office.

Just imagine the benefits for adults and students for these small moments of connection with the natural world.

From Health to Confidence

Taking care of our most basic needs is crucial for everyone, but especially those of us who spend our lives serving and supporting others.

Nobel Prize–winning advocate Malala Yousafzai knows this all too well. In reflecting on the demands of activism and advocacy work, she says, "You can get tired. Exhausted. So what you need to do is give yourself a bit of time to actually reboost yourself with energy. Along with that, you need to make sure you eat good food, you drink enough water, you don't dehydrate yourself, and you have yourself a good sleep" (n.d.). She then acknowledges that she doesn't always do all of these things. "I'm very bad at hydrating myself and with sleep, but these are the things that I know are important, and I'm told many many times to do it, and I remind myself to do it. It's very easy to forget about it because you're just so busy in your work that you don't look after yourself" (n.d.). But she continues to work at self-care because without taking care of herself, she won't get to do the important work that she's called to do. Just like us, she won't be perfect. But we can all keep striving for balance.

Like the foundation of a building, our most basic needs such as nourishment, hydration, and rest are vital. If these are shaky, we're going to struggle to just get through each day, let alone have the energy and zest needed to provide an amazing learning experience for students.

But these aren't the only needs we have. In the next chapter, we'll dig into two important intrinsic motivators—psychological needs we all have—competence and purpose. If your confidence has felt shaky, it might be time to recover your swagger.

3

Recover Your Swagger

"When you know your why, your what becomes more impactful because you are walking towards or in your purpose."

—Michael Jr.

Think back to the story I shared in Chapter 1 about my own struggles as a teacher. One of the biggest factors in my growing sense of burnout was a loss of confidence. Every year I felt like I couldn't teach everything I was supposed to. Whole units fell by the wayside or got chopped way back. As testing took up more and more time—along with extra meetings and new district initiatives—my sense of purpose faded. As my confidence ebbed, my stress increased. I was so focused on the *what* and the *how* of my work that I didn't pay enough attention to the *why*.

As it turns out, what I was experiencing was normal and predictable. When these two key intrinsic motivators, competence and purpose, are diminished, our confidence slips and our motivation drops.

Competence and Purpose

There are so many factors that contribute to someone's health and happiness at work. And this isn't just true of educators—this is across the board in any profession. Our sense of belonging and connection with colleagues, the physical environments in which we work, the relationships we have with supervisors, and the sense of purpose we feel for our work are all important factors. But there's one element that is perhaps more important than any other. Without it, even if all else is fine, we will eventually burn out. It's a sense of competence.

Self-efficacy is our perception of our own competence. At the most basic level, when we reflect on our work, do we feel like we're able to be successful? This is so important because teachers who believe they're good exhibit all kinds of positive professional qualities. They are more persistent, work harder, have more enthusiasm for teaching, are less critical of students who make errors, have more goals and aspirations, are more open to new ideas, and have a greater commitment to teaching (Tschannen-Moran & Woolfork, 2001).

Yet this can be so elusive. Our work is overwhelming, and we feel like we can never get caught up. Most of our students might be learning and growing, but it's so hard to see that growth on a daily basis because it is often so incremental. Not to mention, we tend to dwell on students who we're struggling to reach or who are chronically disengaged. They take up a lot of our headspace, don't they?

All of this was challenging enough *before* the pandemic hit. Suddenly, layered on top of everything else, teachers had to learn entirely new tech platforms and had kids who didn't turn on their cameras. Community members blamed schools for not doing enough. Then came the added pressure of dealing with students' "learning loss."

Part of my early research into the subject of professional engagement entailed interviewing career changers. They left other careers, which often paid more money and had more flexible time, to become teachers. When asked why they made the switch, every single one of them mentioned something about purpose. One was the director of a local newspaper and wanted to more directly influence kids' lives in his community. Another had worked in the business world, but making money wasn't fulfilling after a while. They wanted a job that had a greater sense of purpose and connection to others.

This is so important. When our daily work aligns with our vision and mission, even hard days can be fulfilling. The beginning of the school year is often a time when daily teaching is frustrating. You're working at getting routines established, and students' school stamina is low, but filled with a vision of how good things will be soon, you can power through and work at being consistent as you build the foundation necessary for a great year.

How do we feel a sense of competence and a sense of purpose when they're hard to come by? How do we help boost these qualities when the going gets tough?

You Can't Do It All, So Prioritize

One of the reasons I was burning out as a teacher was a growing sense of incompetence. I couldn't figure out why I was always so far behind with work. I felt like my students and I worked diligently, yet every April, I was having to cut whole units that I didn't have time to teach. (*I guess we're not getting to Rocks and Minerals this year!*) Where did all the time go? Was I really so incompetent that I couldn't get to all I was supposed to teach?

This prompted a thought exercise. For an entire year, I kept track of all of the time that was taken away from my teaching. Every time my students had a fire drill or a bus evacuation drill or I was pulled out of class for an IEP meeting, I logged the time lost on a simple file on my computer. Every time we attended a whole school assembly, missed a half-day for a delayed opening because of snow, or had an extra chorus practice to get ready for a concert, I logged the time lost. Some of these activities (e.g., assemblies and concerts) were good uses of time—educational and important. I wasn't logging *wasted* time but *time that I didn't have* to teach reading, writing, math, science, and social studies. I didn't log time spent traveling to lunch or specials (which felt too nitpicky) or time I chose to do something non-curricular (e.g., an extra recess on a beautiful May afternoon). My goal was to see what time I was losing that I couldn't control.

The results were astounding. Over the course of that school year, I recorded 9,021 minutes of teaching and learning time lost. The number was too big to wrap my head around. Here's another way to think of it. We had a six-hour school day: students arrived between 8:45 and 9:00, the school day went from 9:00 to 3:00, and then dismissal was from 3:00 to 3:20. Each day we had lunch and recess for 45 minutes, and my students attended a special-area class (music, physical education, art, computer lab, and library) for 45 minutes. So (not counting transitions walking to and from) we should have had about 4.5 hours of teaching and learning time each day. When you convert 9,021 minutes into 4.5-hour days, you get an incredible 33.39 days of school. That's more than a sixth of the year! See Figure 3.1 for a complete breakdown.

Then I wondered—how much time was I supposed to teach? Expectations were handed out from various people and groups. Our school-based literacy team was encouraging 5th grade teachers to spend 60 minutes a day reading, 45 minutes a day writing, 15 minutes a day engaged in word study, and 15 minutes reading aloud to the class. Our

Figure 3.1 Total Time Lost in One School Year

Activity	Total Minutes	Number of 4.5-Hour Instructional Days
Band	1,260	4.67
Chorus	1,640	6.07
Literacy PD	310	1.15
Early release for PD	600	2.22
Early release for holidays	600	2.22
Morning announcements	900	3.33
Afternoon safety patrol	900	3.33
Delayed openings (snow)	600	2.22
All school meetings	125	0.46
Other assemblies	440	1.63
Guest speakers	170	0.63
Safety drills	41	0.15
Artist in residence	65	0.24
Nurse visits (scoliosis, hearing, etc.)	15	0.06
State testing	255	0.94
End-of-year trips/assemblies	720	2.67
Meetings/trainings	320	1.18
School pictures	30	0.11
Book fair	30	0.11
Total	**9,021**	**33.39**

math specialist said we should spend an hour a day on math. Across the school we were trying to carve out 20 minutes each morning for a morning meeting. Forty-five minutes was the understood amount of time to spend on science and social studies each day. When you add these expectations up, you get 5 hours and 5 minutes of time we were expected to teach. But when you factor in the 33.39 days we lost, we actually averaged only about 3 hours and 40 minutes a day (see Figure 3.2). That's right—we only had about 80 percent of the time we needed. No wonder I felt so incompetent!

What's even more disheartening (there's a silver lining coming, I promise) is that you likely have more to teach and less time to teach it

Figure 3.2 Actual Teaching Time

Expected Daily Instructional Time	Supposed Daily Instructional Time	Actual Average Daily Teaching Time
5 hours and 5 minutes	4 hours and 30 minutes	3 hours and 40 minutes

than I had during the 1999–2000 school year. Local, state, and national testing surely takes more time than it did back then. You know that over the past few decades, more content and initiatives have been added to schools while few have been taken away.

What's the silver lining? You likely can't actually get to everything you're supposed to. It's not your fault. It's not that you're incompetent. No one can teach 5 hours and 5 minutes of content in 3 hours and 40 minutes.

Instead, prioritize. What are some things you can take off your plate? (If you don't pick something to take off, something really valuable is going to fall off.) For me, this is when I stopped caring so much about homework. It's not a high-impact practice in elementary school, anyway. I still had to give it—we had a school policy requiring me to do so—but I stopped spending much time on it. This was also when I stopped spending time on cursive writing. We had an archaic school expectation that wasn't in any standards that 3rd grade teachers taught students how to write in cursive, 4th grade teachers reinforced it, and 5th grade teachers required it in daily work. Then kids went to 6th grade at the middle school where it wasn't used at all. That was something I could stop spending time on.

What can you prioritize? Can you think of a few things that you and your students spend time on that you can quietly let drop off of your plate? It's better to do fewer things really well than to do too much poorly.

Set Goals That Support Competence and Connect with Purpose

Of course, one of the ways to *feel* more competent is to actually *become* more competent. Good goals can help you get there. So what exactly are *good goals*?

Good Goals Align with Your Purpose

Too often, the professional goal setting that we go through as part of our annual review process feels forced and inauthentic. It doesn't have to. Make sure that the goals you take on feel personally relevant and important. What do you care about? What can you get excited about? Even if your school is taking on a new program that you're not thrilled about, can you find a way to set a goal connected with that program that still feels meaningful?

For example, let's say your school is adopting a new literacy curriculum that spends, in your view, too much time on shared texts—times when all students are reading the same thing at the same time and in the same way. You care deeply about differentiating learning and supporting authentic engagement with your students. What if you took on a goal of giving small moments of choice for students within the lessons provided? Or what if you found a couple of alternative texts so that students could choose one that is good for them?

At one high school where I worked, a small group of teachers decided to work at offering more academic choices to their students. A couple of them especially wanted to push back on the notion that as content becomes more complex, students seem to get less choice. Their work was innovative, students' energy for work increased dramatically, and this group of colleagues was so excited about their work.

Good Goals Are Concrete and Realistic (Perfect Is the Enemy of Good)

"I want to be the best teacher I can be!"

"My goal is to have all of my students exceeding expectations!"

"I will be successful if all of my students are reading at or above grade level by the end of the year."

Goals like these might feel inspirational in the moment, but they can be problematic for a couple of reasons. First off, they're likely unattainable. How could you ever be the best teacher you can be? Can't we always get better? When goals are out of reach, we'll always fail. Goals that ensure failure aren't helpful. In fact, they're going to demotivate you in the long run. Another problem with these goals is that they focus on outcomes that are at least partly out of our control. Imagine that your goal is to have all your students reading above grade level by the end of the year. There are certain factors you can control, such as the quality of instruction, the amount of time students get to read in school, and the availability of high-interest books. You can't control whether students come to school consistently, whether they read at home, or how much sleep they get each night, which are also factors that can affect reading progress.

Instead, set goals that are concrete, realistic, and focused on what you can control. (We'll return to this idea in greater depth in Chapter 6 when you'll be invited to create a plan to support professional engagement and balance.) For example, if you want to help your students become better readers, perhaps you could set a goal of increasing the amount of independent reading time you give to your students each day. Just 10 extra minutes a day would be 1,800 extra minutes in a school year—a significant amount. Want to improve your relationships with students? Set a goal of learning three personal pieces of information about each student in the first month of school. Want to write a blog to connect with educators beyond your school walls? Set a goal of writing one blog post every two weeks. Spend one week drafting and playing with ideas and the second week revising and refining.

When we reach goals that we've set, we get a rush of satisfaction and a sense of accomplishment—a strengthening of our efficacy. This helps boost our senses of competence and purpose.

Write Mission and Vision Statements

When I was a relatively young teacher, I was getting ready to move. One of the things I did to prepare for the application process, especially interviews, was to create a professional portfolio. I collected pictures of student work and wrote short vignettes describing learning experiences from my classroom that I wanted to highlight. I also wrote a brief one-page introduction to each section, stating my philosophical beliefs about the teaching of each subject.

There were two big surprises that came out of this exercise. The first was that I hadn't expected to get such a jolt of energy from writing the belief statements. It was truly invigorating to articulate what I believed. It was also confirming when I had student work samples and stories to illustrate how I was following my beliefs in my teaching. This simple exercise boosted my sense of competence and sharpened my sense of purpose.

The second big surprise was that I also discovered a few discrepancies. For example, while I wrote about how I believed that math in the upper elementary grades should be hands-on—that kids should have lots of chances to use math manipulatives to keep the increasingly abstract concepts such as fractions and division concrete—I had drifted away from this in my practice. *Yeah*, I thought. *Why have I not been using base 10 blocks to help students understand division this year?*

This, of course, prompted me to get back on track. I immediately began blending this into the coaching with my student teacher, and when I stepped back into the classroom, I worked at bringing the reality of my classroom back in line with my beliefs. This was also incredibly reinvigorating.

Focus Your Attention on Positives (Feed the Right Wolf)

What's interesting about the relationship between competence and stress is that it's *perception* that matters. If you're a bad teacher who thinks you're good, you'll likely be happier at work than a fantastic teacher who thinks you're not. And in my experience, there are way more of the latter out there. Even when someone else pays us a compliment, we push it away. A colleague pops into your room for a few minutes and later in the day comments, "Your students were so focused and engaged today!" Instead of saying, "Thanks," and feeling a warm glow, we deflect. "Oh, you should have seen them later on, though. They all fell apart."

Maybe we're nervous about appearing prideful. We're taught to be humble and to not put ourselves above others. But what's the cost? By not allowing ourselves to acknowledge our successes, we may diminish our actual sense of competence.

In a powerful Native American story, a grandson tells his grandfather about another boy who did him a great injustice, and the grandson is furious. The grandfather replies that he, too, gets upset with others who have done him wrong. But he warns, "Inside of me there are two wolves who are fighting. One is full of anger, hatred, envy, and self-pity. The other is full of light, harmony, and peace. Each struggles for control of me." The grandson asks, "Grandfather, which wolf will win?" The grandfather replies, "The one that I feed."

It seems to be human nature to focus on what's going wrong or what might go wrong. I've heard this explained in evolutionary terms. Thousands of years ago, it was more important to not be eaten by a bear than to find the best carrots. Our mind fixates on problems, threats, or dangers—making sure we don't get eaten. In psychology, this is called negativity bias. You've experienced this. You're driving on the highway, and most people are driving safely and responsibly. A few, though, aren't. They're weaving around other cars, nearly hitting several. A few people veer into your lane as they text and drive. When you get to your destination, you're more likely to remember the few bad drivers who made you nervous than the vast majority of your fellow motorists who were civil and safe. "Everyone's driving like they're playing Mario Kart!" you declare when someone asks you about your drive.

Negativity bias can also play out at school. Your class is at an assembly in the cafeteria. Three students are whispering and joking when they should be listening to the music performance. Two students keep trying to be the last one clapping during applause, which feels rude and obnoxious. You keep trying to catch their eyes, but they're too focused on each other to notice you, and to get up and move them closer to you would be even more disruptive to the performance. Twenty of your 25 students are being respectful and enjoying the performance, and you seethe as most of your attention goes to the 20 percent of the class being disrespectful. By the end of the performance, you're furious and embarrassed. You may feel like your entire class was rude.

This sort of thing happens all of the time.

During your commute home from school, the real or perceived failures and frustrations of the day swirl in your mind. A lesson bombed this morning. A colleague made a snide comment in your direction during your PLC meeting. A parent was upset about their son's grade, and even though you made Herculean efforts to help their son get caught up at the end of the semester, they blamed you in a strongly worded email. We churn on these negative events, working them over and over again in our minds.

Yet there were lots of good things that happened as well. One lesson bombed, but four others went quite well. You had a great discussion with a colleague and are excited about a unit you're going to co-teach. You bumped into a parent in the grocery store, and they thanked you for helping their daughter enjoy school so much this year.

Now, of course, we need to have our eyes and ears on students struggling with respectful behavior so that we can help support them moving forward. But we need to be careful that we don't lose sight of all the good that's happening, too. I see this frequently in schools I work in. As I begin work with a school, I'll often have a day or two to observe. I visit classrooms, talk with students, and meet with faculty. It's not uncommon for me to hear some staff saying things like, "Our students have become so disrespectful in the last few years. I would never have dreamed of talking to teachers the way they talk with us!" But when I actually visit classrooms, I see most students engaged and respectful. With the benefit of emotional distance and while not needing to facilitate the learning in the room, I can get a more balanced sense of what's happening. Did I see one student melt down? Absolutely. Did I notice the two kids fooling around in the back of the room? Definitely. Did I see a student sleeping with her head on her desk by the window? Yep. But I also saw several groups of students working hard and engaging in deep thinking. I saw a student pick up a pencil for a classmate who just dropped it. I saw kids laugh when the teacher cracked a corny joke and furrow their brows in concentration as they read a challenging science text.

What if we could honor these events in our minds while acknowledging negative ones? What if we could keep negative experiences in their proportional place?

Here's a challenge to try. Practice training your focus on what's going well—feed the right wolf. As you scan the class in the middle of a lesson, let your attention linger on students who are listening respectfully, not just on the one whose attention is wandering. As students are working at tables, and you're circulating and coaching, notice the groups that are focused and engaged.

Here's another way to practice noticing positives. At the end of a class period, make a simple tally in a three-columned chart. Pick a learning trait to focus on. Engagement. Focus. Respectful communication. Anything. Then replay the class period in your mind. How many students were really engaged (or focused or respectful), somewhat engaged, or disengaged? There's a good chance that more students are somewhat and really engaged than it felt like while you were teaching. The more you direct your attention to positives, the less of a hold the negatives will have on your energy and emotions.

Keep Your Chin Up When Politics Disrupt Teaching

The early 2020s have felt like a return to McCarthyism in the United States. Some states have enacted laws discouraging open discourse about race and racism. Many districts have had to engage in lengthy free speech battles as people (often from outside their own community) work to ban books that have topics or themes that some find uncomfortable. Some states and districts have even been banning efforts to support social and emotional learning, under the ridiculous notion that it's part of a conspiracy to indoctrinate children in critical race theory. These are knee-jerk reactions to terms that have become politicized—not because people in these states don't want children to learn skills of cooperation, empathy, and perseverance. Most agree that these skills are critical for students' success both in school and out.

If you're in one of these places, what do you do? This can be especially tough if part of your purpose has always been to do your small part to help create a more just, free, and accepting society—one where people of all walks of life have lots of opportunities and the ability to thrive. You could, of course, leave. According to a 2024 *Education Week* article, you wouldn't be alone. Book bans across the United States are driving some teachers from the classroom (Heubeck, 2024). You could look for a community more in line with the goals you have as an educator, but this might not be a realistic option for you. Besides, this then robs your district of your courage, passion, and expertise—attributes they clearly need. So how do you navigate these tricky waters? How can you maintain a strong sense of purpose? What do you do when sensitive conversations come up with students, colleagues, parents, or community members?

I posed this question to a friend and colleague, Erin Jones. Erin has been an educator for decades, first as a middle school teacher and then in a variety of roles, including Assistant State Superintendent for Student Achievement in Washington State and Director of Equity and Achievement for the Federal Way School District near Seattle. She also works as a speaker and consultant. One of her areas of expertise is in helping people have challenging conversations about emotionally charged topics, a topic she digs into in great depth in her book, *Bridges to Heal Us* (2021).

Erin offered three habits that educators can practice and an additional idea to consider.

Practice Gratitude

Erin begins every discussion she facilitates with a moment of gratitude. She explains that this is a powerful practice that helps create positive neural networks and can "help people see hope instead of devastation."

This can be another powerful antidote to negativity bias. Erin stresses the importance of *practicing* gratitude. Small moments of gratitude here and there are fine, but to really reap the benefits, it needs to become a habit.

Create Brave Spaces

When Erin works with both students and adults, she doesn't strive to create spaces where everyone feels safe all the time. This will be nearly impossible if your conversation about a tricky topic is to have any substance at all. Instead, she strives to create environments that are "safe enough for people to be brave." She leads with her own vulnerability—telling personal stories of a struggle or challenge that help open others up to sharing their stories. She also says that we're all going to mess up sometimes. We'll say something that accidentally triggers someone else. We'll use a term someone finds offensive. She says, "When you mess up, fess up, and move on." Pivot back to vulnerability to set a tone of openness.

Another way to create brave spaces is to get curious about people's ideas that are different from yours. Instead of confronting and trying to convince someone that you're right (or that they're wrong), ask questions. "Can you help me understand how you're seeing that?" Asking questions is another way we can move away from the shame, blame, and guilt that either shut down important conversations or lead people to move into anger.

Pause

We're more likely to say something we shouldn't or react in a way that is counterproductive when we go too quickly. We let the heat of the moment take over, and we respond with anger or fear. Erin suggests practicing exercises in emotional grounding. For example, taking several slow and deep mindful breaths can help lower respiration and blood pressure, soothing our fight-flight-or-freeze response. Erin suggests that you try counting backward in a second language. This effectively shifts your brain from working from the amygdala (emotion) to the prefrontal cortex (rational thinking), allowing you to gather your thoughts and plan what you want to say and how to say it.

One More Important Idea

Erin offered another important piece of advice that can help you still teach with a sense of purpose, even if your school, district, or state seems to be restricting certain conversations. She encourages educators to avoid the charged terminology that sets off people's alarm bells and instead to use terms that are an effective proxy. For example, instead of talking with students about racism or LGBTQ+ rights, you might facilitate a discussion about belonging. How do we create inclusive communities where all members feel a strong sense of belonging? What do people need to feel positive connection with others? Instead of sending home a letter to parents about social and emotional learning, you might instead name specific skills (persistence, work ethic, collaboration, etc.) or use the broader term of "work, study, and life skills." You're still talking about the same things but using language that allows everyone to focus on the content rather than the terminology that might shut conversations down.

Collect Small Successes

When we see our growth and progress, we feel a sense of accomplishment. Just think of the glow of satisfaction you get from cleaning the kitchen or a section of the garage or from mowing the lawn or painting the living room. You can immediately see the fruits of your labor.

These moments sometimes happen in teaching. You have a short conference with a student to help them with a skill, they have a lightbulb moment, and they can suddenly do something new. But these moments are rare. And they're often hard to see.

So find a way of making them visible.

This is a strategy many teachers I've worked with practice in some form or other, and it's yet another strategy for pushing back on negativity bias. Find some way of collecting successes you have along the way. You might use the Notes feature on your phone or keep a simple document on your computer where you jot down one or two highlights from each day. You could even write them on a slip of paper and add them to a jar, watching the jar fill with small victories. You made a breakthrough with a student who has been struggling. You kept your math lesson to nine minutes of direct instruction, freeing up more class time for students to practice and for you to coach and support. A parent thanked you for the work you do. If you jot down two or three highlights from each day, you'll have several hundred positives to reflect on at the end of the year.

Some people keep a box or folder in a file cabinet to save notes from students and families that they want to keep. After a rough day, when you're having a hard time shaking the email from a parent who accused you of not caring about their child (which especially stings because you care so deeply), pull out the folder of nice notes to remind yourself of successes and positive connections you've made.

Become a Mentor or Cooperating Teacher

The first time I was a cooperating teacher, I found my head spinning. I had been teaching for several years, and I was already running quite a few of my practices on autopilot. Many of them were good, but they were becoming unconscious and even unintentional. All of a sudden, with a student teacher in my classroom, I had to explain everything.

There's nothing like having to explain what you do (and why!) to someone else to help you sharpen your sense of purpose. Every time I took on a student teacher or became a mentor for a new teacher in my building, I benefited immensely myself. There's no way to fall into complacency in the classroom when someone is watching you and at any time might ask you, "Why are you doing that?" You may also find, as I often did, that some of your practices need reworking. Having someone else in your room is a great way to refocus on purpose and improve your practice.

Collaborate with Colleagues

It's awfully hard to learn and grow without good feedback. This is true for our students, and this is also true for us. Although feedback systems are built into our professional learning plans, in my experience, they don't work very well. For one thing, they're infrequent. Most teachers get officially observed about once a year if we're lucky. Another problem is that they're usually evaluative. This can lead us to play it safe when they roll around. Instead of taking a risk and trying something we're really curious about, we stick to a lesson that's tried-and-true. This might lead to a good evaluation, but it rarely pushes our growth and development.

Try grabbing a colleague and engaging in a bit of collegial collaboration, where you each pop into each other's rooms for a short observation to help each other grow in your goals. I have both used this as a classroom teacher and facilitated this with teachers as a consultant in schools, and it's powerful when done well.

Here's a simple structure you might try if you'd like to have a colleague, perhaps a grade-level teammate or an instructional coach, give you some support:

- **Step 1: Share a goal.** Make sure your colleague knows what you're working on so that they know what to look for. Keep this specific and observable. For example, you might be trying to keep your direct whole-class teaching short to maximize student work time.

Or you might be working at using less teacher-centric language ("Here's what you're going to do for me next . . ." or "I'm going to give you 10 more minutes to . . .") and instead use more student-centric language ("Here's your next challenge . . ." or "You have 10 more minutes to . . ."). Giving your colleague a clear focus for their observation will help them feel purposeful with their time and help you gather information that you're looking for.

- **Step 2: Schedule and have the observation.** Keep this short. It only needs to be as long as necessary for your colleague to observe you working on your goal. Five to 10 minutes might be enough. Try to find a time your colleague can observe when they won't need someone to cover their class. Can a colleague visit for 10 minutes during their planning block or lunch break?

  The more logistically simple you keep this, the more likely you'll be to follow through.

- **Step 3: Debrief.** Keep it nonjudgmental. Have your colleague share their observations in terms of what they saw, not how they felt about what they saw. For example, "You began your lesson with a short game that seemed to pique students' interest. They seemed really engaged" is observational. "I really liked how you started your lesson with an activity . . ." is judgmental and can feel evaluative. Also, you don't need to have a big discussion. Keep it short and sweet.

Practice That Magical (and So Hard to Say) Two-Letter Word: No

One of the greatest challenges you likely face as an educator is that you tend to take on too much. Are you on multiple committees that require extra time after school or during the evening? Did you get roped into helping lead the spring carnival or being an assistant coach for the field hockey team? It's so hard to say no, isn't it? It can be flattering and can feed our needs for purpose and belonging to be asked to help or take on a new task, but as good as it might feel in the moment to say yes, we need to keep an eye on our long-term health and balance.

When we spread ourselves too thin, we can erode our sense of competence. It bears repeating. It's better to do fewer things well than to do many poorly.

Try this exercise if you'd like to pare things down. Write down all the different roles you have outside your regular role as an educator (see Figure 3.3). Include responsibilities you have that are completely outside school as well. By the way, don't include personal wellness commitments such as running, yoga class, and so on. Those should be nonnegotiable. Once you have your list, reflect on each. How important is it to you? Is it one you should hold onto or let go?

If you find a few things on your list you can drop, make a plan for how and when you'll drop them. Will you finish the semester or season? Will you wait another month to finish a project or specific task? Can you drop something right away? Next, map out how you'll deliver the news to whoever you need to alert. Is email best, or should you have an in-person meeting? How will you frame your decision? In my experience, simple and honest reasons are best. "I have enjoyed the chance to work on this committee, but I'm overwhelmed right now. There are too many things pulling me in too many directions, so at the end of this semester, I need to end my commitment to this group." Most people will understand and respect your decision even if they're disappointed. They may even admire your ability to prioritize and take care of yourself.

Figure 3.3 Inventory of Commitments

Roles and Responsibilities After School	Comments and Notes
Cross-country coach, six days a week through the fall	This is very intense early in the year, but I absolutely love it.
School scheduling committee	How did I end up on this?
Volunteer at Community Supper Table, every Thursday evening after cross-country season	There are tons of other volunteers. This is one I could possibly give up.
Book club, once a month	I needed social connections with friends.
PTO treasurer	I never really wanted to do this.

Before You Say Yes, Consider If You Can Say "Hell, Yes!"

Of course, you're still going to say yes to plenty of requests. But how do you know which ones to say yes to?

Elaine Welteroth (n.d.) is the former *Teen Vogue* editor in chief and is now a multimedia icon. In her MasterClass on designing a career, she acknowledges that especially early on in a career, when you're first becoming established, you're going to work a lot. You're going to take on lots of responsibilities, and you're going to be grinding away. She recommends saying yes to things you can say, "Hell, yes!" to. If you'll get positive energy from being on the report card revision committee or spending a few summer days rewriting the social studies curriculum for the district—if they feed your senses of purpose and competence—do it. However, if you are overwhelmed by the number of hats you're wearing, or if you don't have energy and passion for these extra commitments, it might be time to pare them down.

Dress for Success

We've all heard that *we are what we eat*, but could it also be true that *we feel what we wear*?

Have you ever noticed how the way you dress can influence how you feel? When you put on workout clothes, you feel more ready to work out. When you dress up to go to a wedding, a funeral, or some other formal event, you feel more formal.

When you get dressed for school, does it help you feel more (or less) professional? Do you feel more (or less) confident? I remember fighting this a bit as a young teacher. A colleague and friend of mine who was a generation older than me playfully teased me about dressing well for school. I would often wear shorts and short-sleeved shirts in warmer weather and jeans and casual shirts during the winter. "Anderson!" he'd chide. "Are you going to the beach or school?" He wore nice pants, a button-down shirt, and a tie every day. As it turns out, he was on to something.

Some studies have shown that what we wear can change how we feel and think. For example, when people are given a lab coat associated with being a doctor, their attention and carefulness increase (Adam & Galinsky, 2012). In another more general study, it was found that clothing plays a role in enhancing many positive occupational attributes including responsibility, competence, reliability, work ethic, and efficacy (Kwon, 1994). In short, if your attire is shlumpy, you'll likely feel shlumpy. If you dress well, you feel more professional, and this can boost your actual sense of professionalism.

It should also be noted that what we wear also influences how others see us. Would you feel confident in your surgeon if they met you looking like they were about to go for a hike in a baseball hat, jeans, and a T-shirt? Might you question their commitment to their work? How might dressing too casually play a role in how our colleagues and their families perceive our work? Might we accidentally send the message to our students that schoolwork isn't important if we don't dress professionally?

After several years of gentle nudging from my colleague, I changed the way I dress. Jeans and sneakers are now reserved for weekends, and I've been wearing button-down shirts and nicer pants ever since. There's no doubt in my mind that I feel (and probably act) more professionally as a result. There's an added benefit here. Bryan Goodwin, educator, author, and CEO of McREL International, calls it the Mister Rogers effect: "It's mentally healthy to have a different outfit for work and home. That way, when you get home, you can change clothes and tell your brain it's time to switch out of work mode."

Taking It Schoolwide

Now that we've explored some ideas for boosting your own senses of competence and purpose, let's consider some that might help your whole staff recover their swagger.

Think About How Your School Appears to Others

If we feel more professional and confident when we dress professionally, just imagine how that might appear to others. If we want community members to see us as professionals, if we want citizens to support our schools, both in spirit and with funding, we might consider how we present to the community. This goes beyond just what we wear but can include just about every aspect of how our schools look and feel.

Here's an idea. Have a group of teachers from across the school pretend like they're seeing the school for the first time. Drive into the driveway of your school. Is landscaping neat and tidy? What's the overall look and feel of the building and grounds? Next, enter the building. Is it welcoming? Are people who help you sign in friendly and helpful? Walk the halls and read the walls. What kinds of student work or artifacts are on display? Are they neat, clean, and current or cluttered and outdated? Look at staff who are in the hallways and teaching in classrooms. How do they appear? Are they dressed professionally? Do they appear engaged and excited to be there? Peek into classrooms. Do spaces look inviting and clean? Do students seem interested and engaged? Go into the cafeteria. Walk the playground. Drop into the teachers' room. If you had never seen these spaces before and were trying to decide what kind of school this was, what would you think? Would you want to send your own children to your school, just based on its appearance?

Once you have conducted this informal audit, make a plan. What did you learn about the appearance of your school? What are some strengths? What could be better? How might these improvements not only boost your own sense of pride in your school but also increase community support?

Some schools are taking public relations to the next level. They're dedicating staff to the effort. One district I work with in Maine decided to be more proactive with community engagement. After several years of feeling defensive as a few negative school stories hit the local news, they decided to be more proactive about how they were presenting to the community. They have someone who is teaching in the music department for about 50 percent of the time and using the other half of his time to actively seek out and celebrate successes from across the district with local news media.

Surface Your Shared Positive Beliefs, Then Integrate Them into All You Do

Does your school have an old and outdated mission and vision statement? You've got the poster hanging in the foyer, but no one even remembers how it was created? It might be time to refresh your collective sense of purpose.

Here's a simple process for facilitating this together as a faculty. I've used this process several times with schools, and it can be really powerful. This can be mostly completed during a regular staff meeting of about 45–60 minutes.

1. Have everyone individually write down a list of their positive beliefs about teaching and learning. Encourage people to write them in the form of, "All students should . . ." or "A great school believes . . ." or "Learning should be . . . ."
   - Example: All students deserve to feel valued and respected.
   - Example: Learning should be meaningful and engaging.
   - Example: A great school believes that everyone is on the same team.

2. Have people join in groups of two. Together, using the lists they each created, partners create a new list. Only positive beliefs they both share get added to the new lists. (It's OK for people to have varying beliefs about great teaching and learning. The goal of this exercise is to surface *shared* beliefs.)

3. Have partners join into groups of four. Once again, these new groups create a list of shared positive beliefs. All four teammates need to agree with each belief added to this new list.

4. Have groups of four combine into groups of eight. Repeat the process.

5. Collect lists created by groups of eight. Have a few people (e.g., teacher leaders, administrators, eager volunteers) take the lists and look for beliefs shared by a wide majority of the faculty. (This is probably best done at another time, and it takes another 30 or so minutes.) Have a wordsmith combine them into about three to six shared beliefs. Write them simply and powerfully. ("In this school, we believe that all students deserve to learn in a safe and inclusive setting—where students' individual strengths and interests are nurtured.")

6. Share the final list with faculty and celebrate.

7. Next, make this list of positive beliefs come alive through connecting them to all you do. When looking for a new math program, view it through the lens of your beliefs. When getting ready for the winter festival, be clear about how your beliefs are being lived through the festival. When teachers set professional goals for the year, have each goal clearly connected with schoolwide beliefs. *This* is how these beliefs become more than a fancy poster—through actually using them on a day-to-day basis.

Boost Collective Teacher Efficacy

It's important for teachers to recognize their competence. Perhaps even more important, when teachers know they matter—that what they do is valued and important—it has a significant impact on their collective teacher efficacy (Wilfong & Donlan, 2021). This is no small thing. John Hattie, perhaps the most important and influential education researcher we've ever seen, rates collective teacher efficacy as one of the most important factors in student achievement, with an effect size twice as large as students' prior achievement and three times higher than socioeconomic status and parental involvement and home environment (Donohoo et al., 2018). In short, when a faculty knows that they matter and believe they can do great things for students, students learn more.

Here are a few ways to nurture teachers' collective sense of efficacy in your school.

Offer each other meaningful, concrete, and observational feedback, and avoid generic praise and gimmicky kudos. Most schools have some sort of process where teachers are observed and receive feedback. This might happen through a formal supervision and evaluation process, when administrators visit teachers to offer professional feedback. Some schools and districts have active coaches who work in classrooms with teachers to guide and support professional growth. You might have periodic walk-throughs, where teams of teachers pop into classrooms to assess implementation of a program or strategy you're all working on. Perhaps your school has a system where teachers periodically visit each other to learn from and with each other. A version of this, collegial collaboration, was suggested earlier in this chapter.

Whatever the process looks like in your school, you might consider the kinds of feedback that teachers receive. If no feedback is given at all, teachers who have been observed often feel unsatisfied and may worry that they're being negatively judged. Feedback that's bland and general, even if it's positive ("Great job!"), is like eating a piece of candy. It feels good for a moment, but it's unsatisfying. Judgmental praise ("I loved how you started your lesson with a game!") can set a tone of judgment during observations, increasing people's anxieties about being observed. Positive judgment is still judgment, after all.

Educators crave real feedback that focuses on specific strengths and observations. Some research has shown that "positive verbal support and appreciation of teachers by the people around them increase their self-efficacy beliefs" (Kasalak & Dagyar, 2020, p. 17). It's validating to be seen. When someone notices the positive strategies we're using and shares those with us, it can help us build on our strengths and boost our sense of competence. As a faculty, you might try using language with each other that's observational and specific instead of generic or judgmental (see Figure 3.4).

Importantly, teachers also crave feedback that helps them get better. This is an essential element of helping them recover their swagger—boosting their actual, not just perceived, competence. Help teachers grow their skills through concrete suggestions and supportive pushes. One way to help people stay open (and not become defensive) is to offer three positives and a push after a short observation. If you as a faculty

Figure 3.4 Nonjudgmental Feedback

Instead of Framing Feedback Through Judgments	Try Offering Concrete Observational Feedback
Great job today!	Your lesson was so lively and engaging!
I love how you played a game to start the class!	When you started class with a game, students brightened up and were ready to learn!
Thanks for working so hard.	Your students are so lucky to have you. All of the work you've put into this unit on ecosystems is paying off. Kids are learning so much!

commit to this structure ahead of time, everyone can be more ready to accept both positives and pushes.

For example, here are three positives:

- Students seemed genuinely engaged in today's work. Their energy was bright, and they were talking excitedly with each other as they worked at solving the challenges you posed.
- Speaking of those challenges, they appeared to offer differentiation that matched students' level of understanding. There was a wide enough variety of problems for students to choose from that they all found some "just right" challenge levels.
- The final share—where groups explained what they worked on to other groups—provided a solid consolidation exercise for students.

Here is one push:

- The direct instruction lesson lasted 17 minutes, and some kids started to tune out at about the 10-minute mark. You could shorten your lesson by asking students fewer questions where there's just one answer you're looking for. Then you could get to the activity more quickly.

If it needs to be done, carve out time to do it. Teachers often feel incompetent when they can't keep up with all the "little" things that come their way. There's paperwork to fill out, emails to respond to, phone calls to make, IEPs to review—it's hard to know where to start. It's like when young kids let their rooms get so messy that they can't even start to clean them. Overwhelmed by the sheer volume of all of the little things lying on the floor, they simply hang out somewhere else, avoiding their rooms altogether.

We also often have multiple people sending us things to do. The literacy specialist sends a survey about upcoming professional development. The head of the union needs everyone to add ideas to a Google Doc about negotiations starting next month. The sunshine committee wants to know about everyone's dietary restrictions for the teacher appreciation luncheon. And the principal wants everyone to read a great blog post in preparation for tomorrow's staff meeting. Because everyone is sending just their "one small thing," they often don't realize how they pile up for teachers.

And guess what? We aren't any better at handling these little homework assignments than our students are—and for all the same reasons. Our workday is packed with little (or no) time for tasks that aren't immediately urgent. After school, we need to prep for tomorrow as well as get our own kids to flute lessons and soccer practice, prepare dinner, and maybe reconnect with our partner for a few minutes before collapsing for the night.

One way to reduce teachers' feelings of incompetence is to clear time during staff meetings, PLCs, grade-level and team meetings, and other dedicated times to have people complete these small but important tasks. Carve out time during the day for these things, and people will be able to get them done.

Take some things off teachers' plates: Consider de-implementation. It's an age-old refrain among teachers: "Every year, more and more gets added to our plates, and nothing is ever taken off!" Are there any practices that teachers can let go of? What if your school looked at all the teaching practices and schoolwide traditions you've got on your plates and then came to consensus on which to keep and which to drop?

For example, if you're moving into new literacy practices around phonics and word work, shouldn't teachers stop assigning spelling words and giving spelling quizzes? Is cursive writing still a skill that all students need to practice?

What about homework? What if a commitment was made that teachers and kids would work all day in school and that after-school time was reserved for kids to play sports, have jobs, hang with friends and family, or hang out and relax? How much time are teachers spending creating, correcting, and hassling students about homework?

How about that tradition of the field trip the 7th grade goes on every year? Twenty years ago, it was packed with science content, but after the original team that created it dispersed, the tradition continued without lots of academic meaning. Could you let that go?

What are some practices that your school could encourage teachers to discontinue so that they can spend their valuable time and energy on the practices that are truly a high priority? If you're interested in a text to guide you through this process, I recommend Peter Dewitt's (2022) book, *De-Implementation: Creating the Space to Focus on What Works*.

Avoid initiativitis: When adopting new curricula and teaching strategies, give people time to get good. New initiatives take time to understand. New teaching strategies take time to master. New curricula take time to learn. Few things frustrate teachers more than a steady stream of new initiatives without time to master any of them. "Flavor of the month PD" is how some describe this phenomenon. In districts where this is the norm, it's common to see teachers stop even trying to learn the new thing. "This too shall pass," they say, recognizing that in six months there will be a new initiative and the old one will likely fade away. Why invest time in learning something new if you're never going to get good at it, anyway?

Teachers will also throw up their hands and give up when they're asked to implement multiple new initiatives at once. It's like asking them to learn to juggle and learn to ride a unicycle at the same time. It's overwhelming. Even the most passionate and energetic teachers in a school get worn down by too much new work all at once.

As your school is planning professional learning, make sure to give yourselves plenty of time to master new techniques before moving on to something new. And keep the number of new initiatives low (one at a time if you can). The more time and support teachers are given to adopt new practices, the more successful they will be, and the more open to future professional learning they will become.

From Confidence to Passion

This chapter has explored some ideas for how to help boost our confidence and teach with a greater sense of purpose. In the next chapter, you'll explore two more intrinsic motivators—autonomy and curiosity—and consider how they can help you teach with more passion. Let's think about how you might rekindle your professional fire!

4

Rekindle Your Professional Fire

"I have no special talent.
I am only passionately curious."

—Albert Einstein

Tom Tuscano teaches math at Dodd Middle School in Cheshire, Connecticut, and he's fired up. We're sitting with a team of his colleagues who have all been engaged in a yearlong professional development exploration of boosting students' motivation. We're about to observe in his classroom, and he's explaining what we're about to see.

His class has just finished a unit, and instead of offering a traditional test, he is trying something different. He realized that if students were going to be more self-motivated, they needed to own their learning. He wanted the assessment to feel like it was more *theirs* and less *his*. So he is offering his students several choices of assessments: They can take a traditional quiz, try a Kahoot quiz, complete a partially filled in table of math problems and answers, or choose from a selection of problems of varying challenge levels on a "heat map" worksheet.

We're intrigued. "Will they all choose one assessment?" one colleague asks. Tom responds that he's encouraging students to try at least two. They'll answer a couple of short survey questions on a shared document after each assessment, explaining why they chose that option and how they think it went. "How will you grade this?" asks another colleague. (You *knew* that was coming!) Tom chuckles and shrugs. "I'm not sure. I haven't figured that part out yet." He's clearly excited and a bit nervous about how this experiment is going to go.

We all head into his classroom and watch as he facilitates this unorthodox math assessment with his students. His students respond incredibly well. They are highly engaged throughout the math period and really enjoy having more flexibility in an assessment. They also show high levels of understanding of content—and not all in the same way. What's most relevant to our discussion in this book is *Tom's* level of engagement. His energy is high, and his concentration focused. Why?

Autonomy and Curiosity

As it turns out, Tom was hitting two key intrinsic motivators at once: autonomy and curiosity. His experiment with giving students choices of math assessments stemmed from a question he had. Why was it that when he asked kids how they thought they did on a quiz, they'd often shrug and say, "I don't know"? He wondered if they didn't know how they did because the work was his and not theirs. He made the quiz. He gave the quiz. He corrected and graded them. Would kids feel more investment in their work if they had some choice about it?

Curiosity is a powerful driver. When we wonder about something—when we tap into our professional and personal interests and passions through our teaching—it's hard not to get more emotionally invested in our work. Curiosity can lead us to new insights as we experiment with new strategies.

Autonomy may be even more important. In fact, autonomy might be the most important intrinsic motivator of them all. Richard Ryan and Edward Deci, the creators and authors of self-determination theory, make the compelling case that it's almost impossible to be truly self-motivated without autonomy. (For a compelling account of their work, I highly recommend *Why We Do What We Do: Understanding Self-Motivation* [Deci & Flaste, 1995].) That's right—without power or control over what you do or how you do it, it might be impossible to be truly self-motivated. You can be compliant (even happily so). You can be externally motivated (by pay or pressure from others). But your motivation can't come from within.

This is no small thing. Numerous research studies have highlighted the relationship between teacher autonomy, job-related stress, professionalism, and job satisfaction. As a rule, the more power and control you have, the less stress you experience and the more satisfied you are at work. One study conducted by researchers at the University of Arkansas at Little Rock and the University of West Florida explored these relationships in depth with elementary, middle, and high school teachers. They found that as curriculum autonomy (control of what you teach and how you teach it) increased, job-related stress decreased. General teaching autonomy (control of classroom conduct and on-the-job decision making) is also important. The more of this kind of control you have, the more satisfied you are with your work and the more empowered and professional you feel (Pearson & Moomaw, 2005).

This isn't just true in teaching, by the way. Nurses in intensive care units who have more autonomy have lower levels of stress, deliver better care to their patients, and even have fewer patients who die in their care (Asl et al., 2022). Researchers across professions have also found startlingly clear negative impacts of a loss or lack of autonomy at work. It can make people feel less accomplished (Maslach, 2011), increase burnout (Glass & McKnight, 1996), and lead to a sense of depersonalization (Cordes & Dougherty, 1993). It has even been noted that the phenomenon known as quiet quitting (doing the least amount possible to slide by at work) may result from people feeling overmanaged, which again decreases workers' perception of autonomy (Aydin & Azizoğlu, 2022). Given all of this, it's perhaps not surprising that a lack of autonomy at work is also associated with workers quitting their jobs (Spector, 1986).

Chances are, especially if you teach in an elementary or middle school setting, you've been handed a program or curriculum that you must follow. You've been told that a morning and afternoon recess break is too much because students need more time in seats practicing basic skills. Special education and remedial teachers are scheduled to be in your room (and if you're one of those SPED or remedial teachers, you didn't create the schedule, either) during specific blocks of time, tying your hands when it comes to creating a schedule for your students that is conducive to learning. You know the last block of the day is the worst time to tackle math or writing, but that's when your students receiving services get help, so that's that.

What's heartbreaking and ironic about all of this is that it doesn't have to be this way. Finland revamped their education system decades ago, giving more autonomy and control to local schools (within a clear national curriculum). They emphasize play and choice-based learning at lower grades, give students many outdoor breaks each day, rarely give homework in younger grades, offer lots of project-based learning in upper grades, and spend little time practicing for standardized tests.

Each year, Finland scores at or near the top of the world rankings in the PISA (Program for International Student Achievement) tests, while the United States finishes in the middle of the pack. (For a compelling look at what U.S. educators can learn about teaching in Finland, I highly recommend Tim Walker's book, *Teach Like Finland*.)

So how do you recapture autonomy if it's been slipping away? How can you gain or regain some professional autonomy and bring your curiosity and passions into your teaching? Here are a few ideas to consider.

Reclaim Your Right to Plan

Are you planning the units and lessons you're teaching, or are you following someone else's plan, from either a program or units created by other teachers in the district? How can you possibly get fired up about teaching something someone else created? How can you have emotional investment in your work if you don't have a hand in shaping it?

I was recently planning a reading unit for a class in a school I'm working in. Many students in the class were getting into fantasy and science fiction stories during independent reading, so that seemed like a good starting point for a unit. There were, of course, a wide variety of readers in the classroom, but as a whole, they needed help being more thoughtful as they read. When I conferred with students, they seemed stuck in thinking about their books in fairly shallow and surface-level ways. They retold events from their books, but when I asked deeper questions about character traits or themes, they struggled. I decided to create a fantasy and science fiction unit that would help them dig into these two exciting and overlapping genres. As I imagined students creating profiles of favorite characters, engaging in challenging discussions about which genre a book (or movie) might be (Is *Star Wars* science fiction? It's got spaceships and robots. Or is it fantasy? There's a princess, and it takes place in the past!), I started to get excited. I could feel butterflies in my stomach as I envisioned students getting fired up. (And wouldn't this be the perfect educationally valid reason to watch *The Princess Bride* with a class?)

If we're going to teach with fire and passion, we've got to reclaim our right to create our own plans. If someone handed me the very same unit that I created, I would struggle to teach it with as much passion or depth, because I wouldn't have spent the time and energy wrestling with the unit.

Exercise Your Autonomy While Planning

Perhaps you're intrigued by the idea of flexing your creative muscles, but you're wondering where to begin. Here are a few ideas to get you started.

First, Be Clear About Learning Outcomes

Let's say you're going to rewrite a math unit about measurement. The unit you have used in the past is pretty dry, and you want to make it more engaging. You have a vision of students moving around the school and actually measuring things (instead of reading a text about other people measuring) and solving problems.

Before you get too far, make sure you're clear about the learning outcomes for this unit. Make sure that whatever you cook up hits those same objectives and that the assessment you design measures those objectives. Having autonomy about teaching doesn't mean that we can disregard standards.

Be Curious

Tom Tuscano, whom you read about at the beginning of this chapter, began his quest to offer students more choice in summative assessments with a question: "Why do kids seem so disconnected from quizzes? Every time I ask a kid, 'How do you think the quiz went?' they respond, 'I don't know.'" This question led him to a hypothesis. Maybe students can't explain how they did on a quiz because they didn't have any ownership of it. This led him to experiment: Maybe if students had some choices about how they show competence, they'll be more connected with and invested in assessments.

What questions do you have about your students' learning or your teaching? What do you wonder about? What are you curious about? How could you test your hypothesis? What might you try?

Connect Your Passions with Your Teaching

What do you love to do outside school? Is there a way you could bring that into the classroom? Perhaps you love quilting. What if students all got to create a quilt square to demonstrate geometric principles or a scene from the American Revolution? Do you enjoy video production? Could you make a video with your students about chemistry or the class novel you're reading?

Another way to bring your passions to school is to consider hosting an after-school event for students. I once ran a baseball card collecting club as an after-school club. My daughter started on her journey toward veterinary medicine thanks to an after-school dissection that one of her middle school science teachers offered. Would you enjoy hosting a before-school knitting club for students? Or how about a sculpture class on Friday afternoons?

Cocreate Learning with Your Students

One year I had a class that really struggled with engagement. If one kid whispered, "This is dumb," the air went out of the whole class, and we were cooked. I tried fighting them, trying to force them to care about what we were doing. That didn't work—they just resisted more. I tried putting on song-and-dance routines, pouring tons of energy into making learning seem fun and engaging. Sometimes it felt like the harder I tried, the less they cared.

I eventually started inviting them to help come up with ideas for how to tackle content. It was amazing to see their energy for learning when they had a hand in shaping it. We created our own documentary (à la the Ken Burns documentary *Lewis & Clark: The Journey of the Corps of Discovery*) in social studies. We created a safari in our classroom to teach other students about world ecosystems. They even had the idea of having a short "comedy hour" (really only about 10 minutes) before lunch on Wednesdays where students could tell jokes, with the agreement that they would try *not* to crack jokes during math lessons.

So if you're struggling to come up with ideas for how to make learning more meaningful and engaging, you might try asking students for their ideas!

Get Creative with Scripted Programs

You might not have a choice about using a particular program. Your school or district may require everyone to be on board with a specific curriculum. I've been there. It's tough. But it's not hopeless. There are some ways you might still be able to take what you're given and make it better.

Use the Program as a Springboard

Take a look at an upcoming unit. First, be clear about the main learning objectives. Before you tinker with the unit, make sure you're still covering the same big ideas and skills. Next, identify what's good. What are the parts of the unit that are strong? Which elements will your students find engaging? Then, play around with making it better. This might mean making a few tweaks, or you might try rewriting the whole unit.

Shorten the Direct Instruction Portion of Lessons to Increase Student Engagement

In my experience, most programs and curricula written for teachers often have too much direct instruction. It's not unusual for lessons for young children—as young as 2nd grade—to be written to include 30 minutes of direct instruction. Not surprisingly, even teachers with heroic amounts of enthusiasm can only hold students' attention for half of this—leading to inevitable dysregulation and behaviors labeled as "misbehaviors."

Not only do long lessons lead to dysregulation, they're also a colossal waste of time. Because most students can't hold their attention for very long, whatever teaching is in the back half of the lesson is likely lost. This also means there's little time left for students to actually do work themselves, such as practicing skills and applying new learning.

Can you take a 30-minute lesson and make it 20? How about 15? Or 10? If you leave plenty of time for students to work, you can circulate and coach—supporting students who need extra help without trying to make sure all students get it before ending the lesson.

Add Student Choice

A group of 3rd grade teachers was exploring how to make their scripted phonics program better. As they examined a lesson they were about to teach, one of them made the observation that she had a couple of games she used to play that worked on the same phonics skill. Another teacher had a different activity she used to use. Together, they made a quick list of three or four different games and activities that all hit the learning target from the lesson in their program. They then taught the lesson as it was written, but instead of having all students practice the skill the same way, they offered them choices of how to practice. Not only did student engagement go up, but the teachers' engagement was higher—because their planning had boosted their own sense of ownership and autonomy.

Break Free from Your Own Prison

No doubt, we have less academic freedom than we did several decades ago. But there's a second way we lose autonomy that we should have our eyes on. This time, the culprit isn't some "other"—it's ourselves.

Is there a chance that you have more freedom and autonomy than you think? Some school leaders have gone too far with mandating scripted programs and requiring consistency to the point of insanity (I've heard of principals requiring daily schedules and lessons to be posted outside classroom doors and standing in doorways with stopwatches to time teachers' lessons), but this is rare.

In my experience, administrators usually want a more nuanced approach to these curricula. Usually, the expectation is that teachers follow the general scope and sequence of programs while adjusting for the needs of students. I've talked with many administrators who encourage their teachers to tinker with the curricula they've been given, only to hear those very same teachers complain that their hands are tied by those programs. If your administration has given you permission to adjust lessons and units, believe them—and run with it.

Sometimes, teams of teachers create their own prison. This is often the result of cooperative planning in which a team plans a unit (or even a whole semester or year) together in an attempt at creating more consistency for students in a school. Consistency is good, up to a point. Having common goals, methodologies, and assessments can help teachers collaborate and think deeply together and can help ensure that students are all receiving a high-quality learning experience. This can go too far, though. If you get to the micro-level, where every lesson is planned out in fine detail—where the scope and sequence is rigid and uniform—you've essentially created your own scripted program. Now teachers' individual ideas and personalities are stifled, and you may neglect the needs of the actual students who show up in your room. You know each class of students is different, so they'll likely need different amounts of time to complete certain goals. Or a student in one room throws out an idea that takes the learning in a slightly different direction. As you plan with colleagues, consider balancing consistency with flexibility. You might even create units that offer suggestions and options for teachers that encourage flexibility and student-centered teaching. In this way, you can have consistency without sameness.

Don't Outsource Your Planning or Teaching

I worry a bit that we in the profession have been overemphasizing the idea of making teaching simple and easy. Perhaps in an effort to combat stress in teaching, we have accidentally given the impression that teaching shouldn't be hard.

News flash: It's hard. And I don't think we should make it otherwise.

Of course, we don't want it to be overwhelming or so burdensome that we don't have time for health and balance. We also don't want to spend our time and energy on trivial tasks or ones that don't have worth for our students. But we should engage in deep thinking, which requires time when the work is important.

What do I mean by outsourcing our planning and teaching? It's easy to use online tools to save time in ways that diminish our own emotional engagement in teaching. I've seen this happening more and more in schools recently. Here are just a few examples.

- A teacher passed out a writing rubric to her students that she found on Teachers Pay Teachers. The rubric was aesthetically pleasing with nice margins and a beautiful font. However, it didn't match what the teacher wanted for her students. The rubric had a space to tally points, but this teacher wasn't using points of any kind. The categories didn't align with the criteria that students were working on.

- A 1st grade teacher put up a video of a read-aloud for her students to watch as they ate snacks and she corrected papers at her desk behind them.

- As an energizer, a teacher played a video from Go Noodle that his students could dance and sing along with. The teacher stood to the side of the students and half-heartedly danced along.

- A teacher used the online resource toolkit provided by the reading program and had a text-to-speech program read a story aloud to her students instead of reading it aloud herself. The voice was flat and robotic, and the students were clearly bored.

- A math program comes with videos of teachers teaching math lessons. The actual teacher plays the video for students and then directs them to work on a set of problems. When students are ready, the teacher plays the next instructional video.

Sugata Mitra is the education scientist who is the architect of the famous Hole in the Wall experiments in India. The experiments showed that when children were given access to computers and the internet, they could teach themselves to do incredible things. He's an advocate of using technology to support students' learning and is sometimes asked if he believes that computers should replace teachers in the classroom. In a TED Talk about the subject, he related a quote by Arthur C. Clarke: "A teacher that can be replaced by a machine, should be" (2010). His point is that teaching is (or should be) more complicated than following an algorithmic set of directions. It requires dynamic engagement between teacher and students—something that recorded videos and computer programs can't deliver.

Of course, the outsourcing of thoughtful planning has been going on for decades and isn't just about online programs and tools. Basal reading programs and textbooks have long been a source of frustration for teachers who know they can plan and deliver instruction more effectively for their students than people who have never (and will never) meet those students.

What's lost when we outsource our planning and our teaching? When we put up a video of a read-aloud or an energizer, we miss the chance to build relationships with our students. When we're not making eye contact with students as they ponder a story, we miss the chance to share a knowing look with a student who connects with the book. We lose the chance to be the ones who dance, sing, and get silly with our students— modeling how to let your guard down and take a risk in front of others, building trust and a sense of community.

And when we search for lessons or handouts on Teachers Pay Teachers? Or when we simply Google activities to try with our students or use AI to create a lesson? These might be great time-savers when it comes to generating a permission form for field trips or getting a draft letter to families that you can later refine. But when we use these kinds of tools for significant planning, we miss the chance to think deeply about what we're doing and why. We miss the chance to be creative and to think for ourselves. How can we be emotionally invested in our teaching if we overrely on scripted programs or Teachers Pay Teachers? So use these resources thoughtfully and sparingly. They can be great time-savers, but make sure you don't outsource your important thinking and rob yourself of the thoughtfulness that comes from struggle and think time.

Boost Autonomy and Curiosity Beyond Planning

There are other ways to reignite our passion for the profession beyond effective planning. Here are a few ideas to get you going.

Rearrange Your Classroom

Is there another way to organize your classroom space that might better align with the way you want to teach? Perhaps you want your high school students to have more in-depth whole-class discussions, but they're sitting in rows. You could move seats into a horseshoe or circle so that students are facing each other and not just you, allowing dialogue to flow more freely from student to student. Or perhaps you realize that you rarely sit at your desk, and it's taking up a huge amount of space in the room. How freeing would it be to ditch the desk? How much student workspace would that open up? Where else might you sit and work?

Dive into an Independent PD Project

You don't need to wait for your school or district to provide you with professional development opportunities. You can create your own.

What if you have been using a reading workshop model for years, but others are pushing you to adopt strategies that align with the science of reading? Can you blend the two? What would it look like to do both? What elements of your previous reading workshop model might you minimize or change? What might you add? Are there folks already doing this? If so, what are they trying?

Of course, that's just one example, but imagine how energizing an independent project like that could be. You could scour through blogs, read a couple of books, attend a local conference, all with the goal of exploring a topic you're passionate about. In addition to informing and improving your own teaching, you might then be able to share what you've learned with colleagues.

Consider If It Is Time to Shake Things Up

Though each new year brings its own adventures and challenges, certain aspects of teaching can feel monotonous after a while. If you've been teaching high school English or chemistry for years, grading essays or conducting the same labs over and over can get old. I remember hitting this point in my own classroom teaching journey. I had bounced around teaching 3rd, 4th, and 5th grades, but beyond differences in content and some developmental differences, these grades are pretty similar. At the beginning of the year at about the 12- or 13-year mark, I was modeling for students how to carry chairs safely from the circle back to tables—something my students would need to do often—and I found myself thinking (kind of grumping), *I've been modeling how to carry chairs safely for years now. Don't you know how to do this yet?!* I absolutely loved being a classroom teacher, but I remember starting to realize it might be time for a change.

A sure-fire way to shake things up is to consider a different role, either in your school or district or out of it. Chris Hall has been a middle school ELA teacher for over 25 years, and he's a great one. He's a teacher who is often requested by parents, and when he's out and about in the world, he is often getting a "Hey, Mr. Hall!" from former students. He has been professionally engaged and vibrant for years and even recently wrote an incredible book about teaching writing: *The Writer's Mindset* (2021). But he was feeling worn down. "I love teaching middle school students—8th graders are endearing in so many ways," he told me. But after many years, he started to feel like he was in the movie *Groundhog Day*, where each day, each week, each school year felt too similar. "My teaching parameters were feeling stale, and I needed something fresh. I was still enjoying middle school ELA, but as I looked at the next 10–15 years of my career in education, I wanted to feel rejuvenated and inspired by a new challenge."

So this year, he made a switch, and it was a big one. He is now an elementary school librarian. He was nervous about the move but also excited. We had a brief chat after his first day of school. Kindergartners especially rocked his world, but he's so energized. "Elementary school is so different. Elementary teachers seem to care a lot about bulletin boards," he chuckled. "And I'm so excited!"

These kinds of shifts might sound intimidating, but that's kind of the point. If we're no longer taking risks or trying new things as professionals, we can get stale. Work feels monotonous and we lose our edge. Having worked in preK–12 settings, I can assure you that good teaching is good teaching is good teaching. If you can teach 3rd grade, you can teach 7th grade. As long as you have a curiosity for (and some decent knowledge about) a subject or content area, you can teach it.

Is there another role you might enjoy in your district? Do you know colleagues who have made a big shift and found new professional energy and spark? Perhaps you know someone who moved from the classroom to a role as an instructional coach. Or maybe you know someone who jumped from middle school to high school. Ask them if you can sit down and chat about their experience.

There are bigger shifts to consider as well. At the beginning of my career, I never could have imagined myself working as a consultant in schools, but it has brought such joy and energy to my work (and I still get to be in classrooms working with students!). Is there a local education support agency you might connect with, perhaps to try a bit of professional development support work in the summer to test the waters? Do you know people who have tried other roles in education with whom you might talk?

Sometimes the best way to rekindle your professional fire is to really shake things up.

Taking It Schoolwide

What would it look like if a school community worked to support one another's needs for autonomy and professional curiosity together? Here are a few ways we might keep our collective professional fires burning brightly.

Invest in People, Not Programs

I was talking with a district leader about a reading program his district adopted. It wasn't good. Texts weren't terribly interesting. There was little differentiation happening. Some practices were even developmentally inappropriate (like a 1st grade reading lesson that had students looking back and forth between a screen in the front of the room and texts at their desks, something that's almost impossible for 6-year-olds' eyes). "Where'd the program come from? How was it chosen?" I asked. The leader responded that it was chosen by a literacy coordinator in the district because it was research-based (a claim nearly every program can boast) and "it's so easy to follow that anyone can pick it up and teach it."

And here we see both the promise and peril of programs. The allure is clear. It's so much faster to purchase a program and hand it out than it is to build the skill sets of teachers. But if a program is so easy to use that anyone can pick it up and teach it, how good can it actually be? Why would we even need to hire highly skilled teachers? Is this, perhaps, also part of the appeal? If you put programs in place that anyone can use, does it take the pressure off of finding, hiring, and nurturing high-quality talent?

Resist the urge! We must move away from the factory model of education. Good teaching is so nuanced and complex. Teachers must be able to juggle a vast array of micro-factors as they teach. Each class of students is different. Each student brings their unique set of background experiences, skills, gifts, challenges, and personality quirks. A lesson that works brilliantly with one group falls flat with another. A student has a meltdown during an activity, and teachers need to adjust and adapt accordingly. This is hard work and requires highly skilled people.

When moving through the hiring process as a school, seek out educators who are passionate, curious, and driven. Then take the tens or hundreds of thousands of dollars that you would have spent on programs and instead invest in high-quality professional learning for teachers. Help them gain and hone the skills they need to meet the needs of diverse and challenging learners. Give them the guidance and support they need to collaborate and engage in dynamic planning. Boost their sense of competence and watch students come alive to learning and begin to soar academically.

Recognize That Teachers Need Autonomy to Be Self-Motivated

I was facilitating a leadership retreat for public school administrators. We were digging into how to boost student motivation, and the superintendent kept sharing a favorite quote of his: "We're not filling vessels—we're lighting fires." Though he was talking about teachers' work with students, he could just as easily have been talking about administrators' work with teachers.

One of the most powerful and important ways we can help each other rekindle our professional fires is to make sure teachers have autonomy—at least some—about what we're doing or how we're doing it. Remember that it's almost impossible to be truly self-motivated without some degree of power and control. Teachers, just like students, can be compliant without autonomy, but if we want a faculty who is fired up and energized, compliance won't cut it.

Offer teachers ways to exercise their voice, beyond curricular control, to have real power and control over how the school functions. There are so many possibilities. Here are just a few:

- Principal's advisory committee: A small group of educators, representing faculty from across the school, meets periodically to help the principal make decisions and keep tabs on the pulse of the school.

- Leadership teams: Many schools have teams to support leadership in a variety of directions. There might be teams for social and emotional learning; diversity, equity, and inclusion; academic departments; and more.

- In-house professional development facilitation: Teachers can take turns facilitating staff meetings, leading action-research cycles, or leading other professional development for colleagues. This can allow for teachers' curiosities to shine through as people facilitate and choose to participate in PD that feels especially relevant and important.

- Professional learning communities: PLCs are a great way for small teams of teachers to examine student work and set goals for changes to instruction based on students' needs. When run well, these are active, interactive, and vibrant collaborations.

Offer differentiated professional development choices for faculty. Let's say your school is digging into the complex topic of assessment and grading with the goal of shifting toward more learner-centered and competency-based approaches. This is a tough topic for any school. Some staff are hesitant. Others have been tinkering and experimenting on their own already for years. How can you possibly support everyone in their own learning journey while also moving forward as a united faculty?

Instead of everyone participating in the same training (where some folks will throw up roadblocks, and others will be bored as they revisit what they already know), consider offering a variety of learning paths. Some folks might like to engage in an active and interactive workshop where they can ask questions and talk with an expert in the field. Others might prefer to read a book and talk with others as they read. Could you find an asynchronous course as an option for folks who would rather watch short videos and take notes than read a book? These options could all run simultaneously on an in-district PD day. Then you could have everyone gather for a faculty discussion at the end of the day so that folks can share insights, questions, and yeah-buts with colleagues who experienced different learning structures.

Teachers could all then craft an individual goal for what they want to try, based on the work of the day. Do they want to try offering choice on a summative assessment? Do they want to experiment with competency-based assessments for an upcoming unit? Do they want to further investigate how to translate competency-based assessments into traditional grades (that are still required through your district's learning platform)?

Especially when entering into what can be emotionally charged professional learning, offering educators some power and control—and the chance to make the learning their own—can go a long way toward helping folks move from passive (or active) resistance to authentic engagement.

Balance collaboration and autonomy: discipline and classroom management. A common source of friction in schools centers around classroom management and discipline. A school where all teachers have complete autonomy with discipline can be pretty dysfunctional and confusing for all involved—students, teachers, parents, and administrators. When everyone has their own rules, routines, expectations, and systems for helping kids navigate how to behave in various settings, everyone usually ends up confused and dissatisfied. On the other hand, when schools adopt rigid systems of management—where all teachers are supposed to do and say exactly the same things in the same ways—teachers lose autonomy and become resentful and may rebel.

Work toward finding common ground but also allow for individuality. For example, an elementary school might decide that all teachers will create classroom rules with their students early in the year but can do so using a variety of different methods. That same school might encourage all teachers to spend a good bit of time and energy early in the year setting up routines in their classrooms while creating some consistent expectations for hallways and other common spaces—expectations that all staff and children will follow. A high school might decide on a cell phone policy that allows for consistent understanding and flexibility. For example, the rule might be that cell phones remain packed away during class unless the teacher allows students to use them for a learning activity.

From Passion to Joy

Did any of this resonate with you? How might you support your need for autonomy? How might you nurture your sense of curiosity? If you're looking to regain your passion for teaching, these are two good areas to explore.

And, of course, the ideas offered in this chapter are by no means exhaustive. What else comes to mind for you? How else might you rekindle your professional fire?

Next, we'll dig into two more intrinsic motivators: belonging and fun. You'll explore a bunch of ideas for how to sustain positive connections with colleagues and find more joy in everyday teaching.

Let's consider how you might refresh your spirit!

5

Refresh Your Spirit

"In every job that must be done there is an element of fun. You find the fun and SNAP! The job's a game."

—Mary Poppins

It was late fall one year, and I was about to work with a group of teachers at a school in Virginia. One of them arrived a few minutes early for her session, gave me a quick "hello," and immediately started crunching numbers and filling in data on a spreadsheet. Her brow was furrowed and her concentration focused. I thought she must be poring through recent test data and asked if I was right. She shook her head. "Nope," she replied. "It's scores from our fantasy happy hour league. I'm the commissioner, and I have to get results out by this afternoon."

I laughed and asked for an explanation. (Fantasy *happy hour* league?) In her school, some teachers started a fantasy football league. A few other teachers who didn't like football heard about it and decided to start their own fantasy league based on something they enjoyed. They set up a scoring system, met for happy hour, and kept track of points. If you were the first to arrive, you got points, but if you got there late, you lost points. You gained points for buying a round or getting snacks to share, but you lost them for spilling a drink. The league was inclusive—anyone could join, and nonalcoholic drinks were fine.

What a great example of the old adage about teacher retention: "A staff that plays together stays together."

It's also a great example of a way to meet the two psychological needs that are the focus for this chapter: belonging and fun—two key components in keeping our spirits fresh at school.

Belonging and Fun

In Abraham Maslow's widely cited theory of human motivation (1943), the need for affiliation—for connection with others—is barely less important than our most fundamental needs for food, water, shelter, and safety. If you've worked in a school where faculty are positively connected and enjoy working together, you know what a joy it can be to come to work. Conversely, if you've ever worked somewhere where you feel like you don't fit in—where you struggle to find friends and colleagues you enjoy—you know how demoralizing this can be.

What first brought you to teaching? Maybe it was a deep sense of purpose and a commitment to make the world a better place. For me, those loftier ideals and goals settled in later. What first brought me in was much more basic: joy. When I first started teaching swimming lessons as an after-school job at the local YMCA, I really enjoyed helping kids learn how to swim.

I also have fond memories of my elementary school years as a student. I loved racing in from recess and sliding across the carpet to be as close as possible to Mrs. Mottram as she read a story after lunch. I remember constructing wreaths out of pine cones and wire and putting on a class play. And of course, I remember the intensity and passion of kickball at recess.

These are the kinds of things that first drew me to teaching. I wanted to spend more time in that world. It wasn't until I got to college and started taking education classes that the seeds of being a changemaker in education were first planted. When I saw how some students—especially those with learning disabilities—weren't being served well in school, I became passionate about high-quality differentiated learning and creating classroom environments where all kids could thrive. Teaching with a sense of purpose brought my commitment as an educator to new levels.

But what first brought me to teaching was simple enjoyment. It was fun.

Is any of this resonating with you? Did you also go into teaching, at least in part, because it was enjoyable? And, like me, do you sometimes struggle to hang onto that joy? Do you yearn to connect with colleagues in more positive and powerful ways—to feel like school is a place where you get to spend time with people you genuinely enjoy? Can we still find joy in teaching?

Absolutely. And that's what this chapter is all about.

Make the Academic Work Itself Joyful

A colleague and I were once in a heated discussion about celebrating holidays in school. Valentine's Day was approaching, and I was grumping (old man, get-off-my-lawn style) about how disruptive this day was for my 5th graders. I couldn't stand the way this holiday (along with most others) took our attention away from learning and created stress for students. (Do I have to bring in cards for everyone? Can we eat candy in school? Can we decorate Valentine's Day card boxes like we did in 4th grade? Are we going to have an all-day party?) It all felt like such a waste of time and energy to me.

"Mike!" my colleague pushed back. "Don't be such an old fuddy-duddy! Kids should be allowed to have fun sometimes in school, you know!"

That was the moment I realized our disconnect. I thought everyday learning should be fun. We didn't need a Valentine's Day party to take a break from toiling in the trenches. We were creating a class quilt in our geometry unit in math and working on independent research projects (with tons of student choice and self-direction) in social studies. Students were reading books of their choice in reading workshop and writing poetry in writing workshop. In fact, in lieu of a traditional Valentine's Day party, we were getting ready for a poetry slam on February 14, where students would each read a poem or two of their choice and receive snapping applause from classmates.

Unfortunately, students often don't feel like schoolwork is enjoyable. (Have you heard what some kids say "school" stands for? "Six Cruel Hours Of Our Lives." Ouch.) It's hard to enjoy teaching when our students don't enjoy learning.

It's probably unrealistic to make *everything* enjoyable for all students, but what if we made it our goal, when planning units and lessons, to keep authentic student engagement front and center? When kids enjoy their schoolwork, they learn more, so this isn't just about fun for the sake of fun. Importantly, there's a strong connection between fun and belonging. When you and your students are having fun together, you become a tighter and more cohesive community.

The challenge of exactly *how* to make learning more joyful is a bigger topic than can be handled in much depth here. In case you're interested, two of my other books are all about that very thing: *Tackling the Motivation Crisis* (2021) and *Learning to Choose, Choosing to Learn* (2016).

Still, I don't want to encourage you to "make learning more joyful" without suggesting at least a few ideas for you to consider.

Boost Purpose Through Products, Projects, and Presentations

Kids have more energy for learning when there's authentic purpose driving their work, but sometimes the content itself might not feel full of purpose for students. (Try justifying to 12-year-olds why cinquains or equations involving volume and mass are important.) So give everyone something important to work toward. Can you create a class bulletin board display in the hallway to showcase learning? Can all students contribute written pieces to a class anthology that you'll copy for everyone? Can you make a movie? Can students put on presentations to each other or other classes?

Give Students Choices About Learning

I've been working in an alternative high school program this past year, and teachers have been working at giving students more choice. In one ELA class, the teacher made the shift from using a whole-class novel to allowing students to read novels of their choice. She still teaches whole-class lessons and leads whole-class discussions, but students think through the lens of the books they're reading instead of the one common class novel. One of her students admitted to her that he's reading a new book for the first time since 5th grade. She was actually having a hard time getting him to put it down to join discussions.

When students have some choice about what they're learning, how they're learning, or how they demonstrate learning, they have more positive energy for work. And guess what? When your students have more positive energy for work, it's so much more fun to be their teacher. So let your students choose which novel to read in the English language arts unit about the hero's journey. Give your students a couple of options for how to demonstrate competence instead of requiring all to take the same quiz. Instead of having all students complete all practice problems in a set, let them pick and choose the ones that they think are in their "good fit" zone.

Throw Learning Celebrations

I'm always astounded at the amount of time and energy teachers, kids, and parents will pour into decorating a classroom for Halloween. What if we harnessed that creative energy for celebrations that focused on learning? We could decorate hallways with ocean creatures during a science unit. Students could dress up as favorite characters from books and pose as wax museum statues, explaining their characters as audience members walk by. Students could create short stop-animation movies based on content they're learning and then have a mini film festival to celebrate final products. Let's still throw fun parties in school—let's just make sure the learning is the focus of the fun.

Play Academic Games

In academic programs, games are often an afterthought or a "get to it if you have time" option. Let's prioritize these games. You can create Jeopardy questions to help students consolidate learning at the end of a unit. Students could also create their own Jeopardy answers and questions as you worked through the unit so that they were helping create the game as you went. You can create simple dice and cards games to practice computation skills in math. If you're struggling to find or create a game that fits the content you're working on, invite your students to try coming up with one. I once had a student create a version of dodgeball based on our study of the American Revolution: Patriots Versus The Redcoats.

Sing and Play

Online resources like Go Noodle are a great place to learn songs and games you can play with students, but—for John Dewey's sake—make sure to lead these yourself with your students most of the time. My mother once told me about how singing with her 3rd graders allowed her to make meaningful eye contact with students who she otherwise struggled to connect with. The same holds true for playing games. When I'm leading a group of 1st graders in a round of The Human Protractor or a group of sophomores in a round of Would You Rather?, I can have small moments of connection with students through playful eye contact and fun side interactions. We have to lead this playfulness ourselves to reap the benefits of joy and connection with students.

Plan Collaboratively

There's incredible energy and passion that can come from collaborative planning—when you have control over that planning.

One year, I teamed up with my colleagues, Mike and Andy, to finish the year with a cross-grade research unit focused on nonfiction reading and writing as well as speaking and listening skills. We created trios (a 3rd grader from Andy's room, a 4th grader from mine, and a 5th grader from Mike's) and let them pick a topic they wanted to learn about together. Trios had about five weeks to meet for an hour a day to research their topic, create projects to teach others, and then present to other groups. I think Andy, Mike, and I learned as much and had as much fun as our students did. Was collaborating with colleagues more work? Heck, yeah. Did it make heading to school each day a bit more joyful? Heck, yeah.

Do you have a colleague or two you might collaborate with? They don't need to teach the same grade or content. In fact, variety can make the collaboration that much more interesting and fun.

Connect with Positive Colleagues: Leverage Emotion Contagion

Have you heard of emotion contagion? It's a well-documented phenomenon that explains how people's moods tend to be catchy (Hatfield et al., 1993; Herrando & Constantinides, 2021). You walk into the staff room where people are laughing and joking, and your spirits rise. Or you walk into that same staff room and people are grumping about "kids these days" with furrowed brows and dark scowls, and you feel yourself turn a shade darker.

As social creatures, we're tuned into each other and are affected by how others act and feel. So the question here to consider is, how can you leverage emotion contagion to help refresh your spirit?

Chances are, you've got some colleagues who spend a lot of time complaining. They seem stuck in a negative spiral and can't get out. One teacher described a group in her school of grade-level colleagues who (no matter what topic they're trying to discuss) kept cycling conversations back to students who struggle with challenging behaviors: "They just keep talking about how the rain is wet. And someone took their umbrella."

Chances are, there are also plenty of colleagues in your school who are more positive and playful. They also have students who struggle with challenging behaviors, but they don't dwell on it or they see it for what it often is: developmentally appropriate (albeit frustrating) behavior. They're more likely to have a positive perspective when discussing challenges. "Oh, these 8th graders who need to keep pushing back on authority are on a rip today. It's a good thing I was perfect when I was 13!"

Who do you spend more time with? One thing to be aware of as you mull over this question is that a sense of belonging can be gained through shared positive or negative energy. One of the reasons complaining about kids can be so appealing is that you feel a sense of connection with others as you do it. You get this sense of "we're all in this together," which feeds our need for belonging.

Of course, if you're on a team of folks who tend to grump and grouse, you likely have to spend time with them because you work together so much. But there are other times when you have more choice. Who do you sit with at faculty meetings or during professional learning days? Who do you chat with before and after school? Can you carve out more time for colleagues who bring you up rather than down?

For several years I was on a team with teachers who were absolute soul-suckers. They talked negatively about children, families, and colleagues on a daily basis. They didn't like teaching. When they did joke, their humor was laced with cynicism and sarcasm. My heart sank every time we met for grade-level meetings or planning sessions. So I made a point of going out to breakfast once a week with a friend in another grade who was positive and enthusiastic about teaching. Breakfasts with Cindy on Wednesday mornings were a soothing tonic and critical for keeping my own spirits elevated.

If you want to be a small part of building a more positive and adult culture in your school, be aware of how your emotions are affecting others. When you smile and laugh, you can help spread positivity. More on this later.

Find Colleagues Outside Your School

Sometimes it's hard to connect with others in your school. It might be that your schedule doesn't line up to allow you to eat lunch with colleagues. Or you might be the only Black educator in a mostly white community or the only gay teacher where it's hard to be openly part of the LGBTQ+ community. As a middle-class cis white guy, it's rare that I find myself in this position, but one year in my school there were 78 women and four men—me and the three custodians. There were times I felt out of place.

If you find yourself craving collegial connection and it's not happening in your school for whatever reason, it might be time to look outside your school. Do you have friends who teach in other schools who you could reach out to about forming an online collaboration group? You could meet once a week on Thursday evenings to hang out online, chat about school, and ask each other for advice. You might also connect with an online community of educators. There are plenty out there on a variety of social media platforms. Search around to find some like-minded colleagues and carve out time to attend online sessions.

Combat "Crabs in a Bucket" Syndrome with an Adult Learning Community

Did you know that people who fish for crabs can leave a whole bucket of them unattended without a lid and not worry about any of them escaping? If a crab on top of the pile tries to climb out, the ones nearby grab it and pull it back down.

We see this phenomenon in the workplace as well. Someone shares an idea of something they're excited about trying: "I'm thinking of having my students cocreate the next social studies unit with me to boost their investment in learning and tap into questions they care about!" But someone grabs their leg and yanks them back down: "That's never going to work. Your kids aren't going to care about the stuff they're supposed to learn."

You can combat this syndrome by creating a specific kind of support group. An adult learning community is a small network of like-minded colleagues who want to share and think together. Find a few people in your school or district. Or perhaps reach out to a few long-distance colleagues. Meet on a regular basis to share ideas. You might read a book together or watch a TED Talk and discuss. Have people bring exciting ideas to the group for encouragement and extension ideas.

Small groups tend to be better. During the pandemic when schools were shut down, I was invited to join a small group of consultants for some online meetings to share how we were adapting our work to online platforms and to support each other through a tough time (when most of us had much of our consulting work disappear in a heartbeat). The group was dynamic, supportive, and incredible—for a while. Then, as more people joined, it became unwieldy. It was hard to know everyone in the group, which made it harder to feel safe to share openly. Whole-group discussions became difficult, and subgroups formed, which were hard to facilitate, even for professional facilitators. I eventually stopped going to meetings once the small-group feel had diminished.

Remember to Enjoy Your Students

Our colleagues aren't our only potential source of meeting our needs for belonging and fun. During the whirlwind of a busy school day, it can be easy to lose sight of why we got into teaching in the first place: our students. Let's remember to enjoy their quirky personalities and the funny things they say.

One way to do this is to keep a log of amusing moments that happen through the course of a day. You might keep a separate file on your tablet or have a good old-fashioned notebook you keep handy. When you hear a student say something goofy or adorable or weird, jot it down. Just the other day I was in a 1st grade classroom, and during a transition period one boy turned to another and said in a matter-of-fact voice, "Did you know? Chickens have mohawks."

How can you not love that?

Here's another idea to keep in mind that can keep your energy fresh and positive about your students. There are some predictable characteristics of certain ages and stages. Nine-year-olds tend to be a bit anxious. Twelve-year-olds are talkative. Sophomores swing between being able to have mature conversations to making fart noises and laughing uncontrollably at the drop of a hat. Can you find these characteristics loveable? Can you understand and enjoy the hallmarks of the ages you teach?

I was once working with a 5th grade teacher who was struggling with a behavior challenge. His students couldn't seem to walk through the halls without jumping to try to touch the doorframes as they passed through them. As we worked on this together, he realized why his students were doing this. Many were in the middle of growth spurts. They couldn't reach that doorframe last year, and now they could. The teacher shifted his perspective and decided to put colored dots on the doorframe as targets and teach his kids how to tap them lightly so that the noise wouldn't disturb nearby classes. What a shift! Instead of fighting development, this teacher embraced a quirk of the age and found more humor and joy in his students.

Connect with Your Students

Here's a quick exercise to try that will help you uncover how well you're connected with your students. I first learned this exercise from Don Graves, one of the iconic creators of the writing workshop literacy model. First off, if you teach multiple classes, pick one to start with. Next, take a piece of paper or start a simple doc on your computer and write all of your students' names in that class from memory down the left margin in the order in which you think of them. (Just that is interesting. Who do you think of first? Who do you struggle to remember?) Now, next to each name, write down something positive or interesting that you know about each student that doesn't have anything to do with academics. Tory likes horses. Kody's into skateboarding. Rico is on the football team. Ezra's idol is Roberto Clemente. Don't be surprised if this part is really hard. Certain students are eager to share about themselves, and others are more reserved. Finally, put a checkmark next to that piece of interesting information if you have talked with that student about it recently.

Not only does this activity help surface how well you know your students, but it helps emphasize the importance of students knowing that you know them. If you try this exercise, you'll likely find some gaps. Now you've got your next challenge. Fill in those gaps. Start chatting with students you don't know as well. "Hey, Maria. How was the weekend? Did you do anything fun?" "Mike, you wear a lot of Red Sox gear. Are you a big fan?"

We spend all day with our students. Let's make sure to create strong connections and bonds. It's good for their learning and great for us, too.

Use Humor with Your Students

A teacher felt his 9th graders' attention waning. He paused his instruction and said to a student, "Paige, what is that over there on that wall?" As she turned to look, he remarked to the other students: "Look at that. I just turned the Paige." Students groaned and giggled.

Another way to set a more joyful tone with your teaching—both for your sake and your students'—is to find small ways of injecting humor into the day. Don't worry. You don't need to be a stand-up comedian to bring humor to your teaching!

This is no laughing manner. There's significant research that indicates that humor creates conditions where greater learning can take place (Bryant & Zillmann, 2014; Savage et al., 2017; Ziv, 1988). You may worry that your students will get too silly or even out of control if you joke around. One thing you might do is to help them learn how to handle humor well. A middle school math teacher I was working with did just this. He had inserted goofy pictures of students into problems projected on the board, and students (including the ones whose pictures were projected, importantly, as he had asked their permission ahead of time to use their pictures) would laugh uproariously. He'd let the laughter go a few seconds and then say, "OK everyone, bring it back and let's work through this math challenge." Students would settle in to work on math. By helping students manage their reactions to the humorous pictures, he was keeping the attention focused on the math while also helping students practice skills of self-regulation.

Here are a few other ways to use humor in the classroom.

- **Have a joke of the day/week:** Have a spot on the classroom wall where you post a joke that rotates fairly regularly. These might be tied into curricula or not.

- **Be a little punny:** "What did the teacher cry when they jumped out of the paper closet?" "Supplies!" Dad jokes. Groaners. Puns. They're the best. There are dozens of lists of these jokes online. Read through some and find ways to weave them into your teaching.

- **Invite students to share jokes:** I was coaching an elementary art teacher recently, and a 1st grader leaned over to tell me a joke. "Why do golfers wear two pair of underwear?" "In case they get a hole in one." Your students have got lots of jokes to share. I highly recommend having them preview their jokes with you before they share them with the class, just to be safe.

- **Avoid sarcasm:** "Humor" that is meant to knock someone down a peg or meant to elicit a laugh at someone else's expense should be avoided at all costs in the classroom. When a student asks a question that you just answered and you respond by saying, "Oh, that was a brilliant question! Can anyone inform this poor hard-of-hearing soul what they should have heard 30 seconds ago?" You may get a chuckle from some, but at what cost? You've diminished that student's sense of self, broken trust, and decreased the sense of safety you worked to build in your room.

- **Use irony sparingly:** Irony is a close cousin of sarcasm, but without the intent to hurt. When you're ironic, you say one thing by meaning another. "Well! That was the best video I've ever seen!" you might remark after a particularly dry documentary about cell division. There's nothing hurtful about this remark, and irony can be a way to be playful, but it can be confusing for some students. I remember once a student telling me at the end of a school year, "I couldn't always tell when you were joking and when you were serious, Mr. Anderson." Ouch.

Smile More

Do you remember Eliud Kipchoge, the marathon runner from Chapter 2 who runs at a "conversational pace" for most of his training? He's got another trick up his sleeve. He does something curious as he's pushing through the final stretch of a race. When the going gets tough, when he needs to reach down deep and finish strong, he smiles. Why?

As it turns out, science has uncovered a whole raft of benefits of smiling, even when forcing one. Kipchoge knows that smiling triggers the release of endorphins, serotonin, and dopamine and can reduce your perception of effort and pain—helping athletes push through tough efforts with greater energy and performance (Taylor, 2023). It can also improve your physical response to acute stress, help you recover more quickly from stress, and reduce illness over time (Cross et al., 2022). One research study investigating the "Good Samaritan effect" even showed that smiling at someone else can even make them more willing to help others (Guéguen & De Gail, 2003).

Amazingly, smiling can even change your perception of other people's moods and intentions. In one fascinating study, participants who held a pen in their teeth to simulate the muscle movements of smiling rated other people's facial expressions and body movements as happier than control group participants (Marmolejo-Ramos et al., 2020).

Let's also remember the power of emotion contagion—that our moods are influenced by those around us. When we smile, we help boost the moods of others. How might this apply in the classroom? Which of the following two loops would you prefer to be in?

Your students are playing a game and are starting to get a bit rowdy. You can frown and raise your voice. "Excuse me! You all know better than this. You need to settle down, or we're going to shut the game down!" Your frown and negative energy increase your feelings of stress and decrease your ability to manage it. Your negative mood also increases your chances of interpreting students' behavior as negative, which may be accurate because your negative emotion is contagious and can actually darken your students' moods. You and your students are now primed to be less regulated, and the class is likely on their way to a meltdown, which increases your chances of falling back into this same negative feedback loop later in the day.

Or you could also handle this situation with a smile and a friendly reminder. "Hey, everyone. It's getting a bit loud in here. I know you're having fun, but we need to be respectful of the class next door. Bring the volume down a bit." Your smile and positive energy boost your own mood and make this situation feel less stressful. As your students react to your request, you're more likely to view their behavior as positive, which it very well may be because your positive emotion is contagious and boosts their moods. This increases the class's chances of staying in control and has a positive impact on the rest of the day and beyond.

This really makes you question the whole "Don't smile 'til Christmas" adage, doesn't it?

Practice Gratitude

Of course, it's easier to smile when you're feeling positive. What if we could intentionally generate positive feelings? Wouldn't that be amazing? As it turns out, we can, and it's another way we can feed the right wolf.

The research on the correlation between practicing gratitude and happiness is astounding. The simple act of writing down a few things you're grateful for each week can make you feel more optimistic in general. (People who write down irritations instead are much less optimistic.) Writing a letter of thanks to someone increases people's sense of positivity. Expressing thanks to a partner helps people communicate more effectively about concerns (Harvard Health Publishing, 2021).

Did you notice how simple each example was? What if you picked one day a week to jot down a few things you are grateful for or to write a letter to someone you appreciate? What kind of impact might that have on your spirit?

It reminds me of a poster I saw recently in a high school I was working in. It read, "What if you woke up tomorrow and were only surrounded by the things you felt grateful for? What if you woke up tomorrow and were only surrounded by the things you complained about daily? It kinda works like that."

Taking It Schoolwide

When faculty feel connected with each other in positive ways, they are more committed to each other and their school community. Here are a few ideas and suggestions for how a school can build a sense of belonging and fun for staff.

Build Community and Playfulness Through Your Work Together

A mistake we might make when trying to build fun and playfulness into the adult community of a school is to think of this as a beginning-of-the-year activity. Icebreakers and back-to-school potluck lunches are fine, and they can help get the year started in a positive direction, but if we only think of building community in August and September, we're missing chances to keep that momentum going.

In whatever way you help lead your school community, consider everything you do (building the school schedule for next year, preparing for open house night, or reviewing test data) as an opportunity to help colleagues build positive connections and engage in playful and enjoyable work. For example, before groups of teachers start exploring test data, have each team find five commonalities they all share (pets, favorite foods, places they've visited, etc.). Next, have each team name their team based on one or more of those commonalities. Use these team names throughout your work together as you explore and interpret data ("Team Beach Fun has noticed that there was a sharper growth in reading comprehension in the 6th grade than we saw last year").

Leverage Staff Meetings

You might use advisory groups, morning meetings, or daily academics to play games and build a positive spirit with your students. What if faculty meetings provided that same opportunity for connection with each other? In some schools, each meeting begins with a faculty member sharing a game or activity they've used with their students. Everyone plays, having a bit of fun and learning a new game they could play with their own classes.

Interactive discussion structures such as four corners, mix and mingle to the music, and even simple partner chats are great ways to share ideas with each other while having a bit of fun. Teachers could volunteer to facilitate a discussion structure to help colleagues discuss important ideas at faculty meetings.

Design the Faculty Room with Belonging and Fun in Mind

Faculty rooms can be dour, cluttered, uninviting spaces, with all the charm and coziness of highway rest stops. Posters about workplace harassment and minimum wage are front and center. Tables are messy. Supplies and materials are haphazardly strewn on crooked shelves. It's no wonder teachers tend to grump and groan when having lunch in there.

What if your school designed a staff room to be as inviting and cozy as a local coffee shop or bookstore? You can still have the required posters on display, but don't make them the center of attention. Instead, you might have student work samples or current pictures of kids engaged in learning displayed around the room. Leave a few teacher-friendly magazines or newsletters out for folks to peruse. Paint the walls an earthy green instead of a pale blue or off-white. Tablecloths and curtains make a huge difference. Have a "pun of the week" display and invite people to submit ideas for next week's puns.

Remember, just like students, our emotions and behaviors are shaped, at least in part, by our environment. Imagine the power of having a staff room that refreshed people's spirits.

Structure Opportunities for Professional Collaboration

Starting a fantasy league (e.g., fantasy football, basketball, happy hour) is just one way you might structure opportunities for connection and fun with colleagues. You might also create opportunities for professional learning that is collaborative and fun. Start a book club to dig into new professional texts. Create a professional learning team that wants to dig into a topic, share ideas, and ask each other questions. Offer the chance to take an online course together or organize a group that will attend a professional conference and return to share new ideas with others. There are so many possibilities. Keep it low-key, inclusive, and simple, and don't worry if only a few people join. A book club with three people is still a good time for those three.

From Joy to Practical Application

You have now explored four key areas of potential growth you might pursue. In Chapter 2, you examined ideas about foundational health and balance. In Chapters 3–5, you considered ideas for how to boost six key intrinsic motivators: competence and purpose (Chapter 3), autonomy and curiosity (Chapter 4), and belonging and fun (Chapter 5).

But how do you truly change?

After all, haven't we all had grand plans to make a change only to struggle to follow through? How many New Year's resolutions have you watched crash and burn only a few weeks into January? In our next and final chapter, we'll explore a process for making new habits stick. You'll also gain tons of practical strategies for following through on new goals.

6

How to Build Powerful New Habits

"A goal without a plan is just a wish."

By now, you hopefully have an idea about a change you'd like to make. It might be vague (*I want to boost my sense of competence*) or specific (*I'd like to keep track of small successes so I can be more aware of the good work I'm doing*). Hopefully you're also excited about this change—you can feel in your gut that it will be beneficial.

You're also likely feeling apprehensive. After all, how many times have you tried to change in the past, only to have the new habit fizzle out? Change is hard, and there are some common roadblocks that can easily derail our best intentions and efforts. Do any of these seem familiar?

- You're feeling inspired to change, and you take on a goal that's too big. You stick with it for a while, but after a few weeks, you quit.

- You want change to happen right away. You look for a quick fix. You set a short-term goal, check it off, and then end up right back in your old pattern.

- You've got a goal but not much of a plan for how to get there, just a vague notion of forcing yourself. You'll grit your teeth and make yourself change. It works for a little while, but you just can't quite make yourself stick with it.

- After several failed attempts at change, you start to feel like there must be something wrong with you. You wonder if perhaps you're just the sort of person that can't change, and maybe you should just stop trying.

These are all normal and common. But you *can* change. You just need a realistic and practical plan that you can actually commit to and stick with. That's what this chapter will help you do.

There are three components to a plan that will work. You need to (1) create a good goal, (2) use practical strategies to help you set a new habit, and (3) set a timeline for when to check in and reassess (which might mean continuing, changing, or dropping the goal for another). I find that when I am working on a plan, I usually start in that order, but often one part of the plan has me tweaking another. For example, a goal I had this year was to add flexibility to my weekly exercise routine. I thought two days of light yoga or stretching was reasonable. There are usually two days a week I don't run, so I figured I'd add flexibility to my calendar for non-running days. I'd check on progress each week when I tallied my weekly mileage in my running log. I'd help myself stick with this new routine by writing the flexibility sessions into my running log to help me see progress and to hold myself accountable. Once I realized I would use that strategy, I revised my plan and removed the part about using non-running days for flexibility work. I decided that recording sessions in my journal was enough to keep me on track, and I liked the idea of having more leeway with my schedule. Yoga or stretching just needed to happen twice a week, whether on a running day or not.

Here are the three components of a plan in more detail. As you explore these, start thinking of how you might apply them to the change you want to make.

Step 1: Create a Good Goal

Good goals have a few key criteria. First (and in my humble opinion most important), your goal should mean something to you. If it's not personally relevant, if you don't find it compelling, good luck following through. What's a big category that you need to work on? Is there a fundamental need that feels in deficit?

Second, a good goal is specific. It's concrete and measurable. For example, let's say the overall broad category you're working on is competence. You're often frustrated that you can't seem to get to everything you should in a class period. Instead of having a goal of "being better at time management" you might set a specific goal of "keeping direct teaching at the start of a class period to 10 minutes or less." That's something specific enough that each class period you can determine if you've been successful.

Usually, a good goal is also about a routine. Remember the advice from Chapter 1 to focus on the routine of the cue, routine, reward loop? This means we should avoid event-based or benchmark goals. These might be motivational in the moment, but once you accomplish them, you probably haven't built a new routine. Without a new routine, you're likely to end up back in the habit you were trying to shift. For example, perhaps a group of you in your school are working toward building more staff connections and having some fun together. Instead of planning to hold a staff breakfast at the end of next month, what if you decided to host a breakfast near the beginning of each trimester or quarter? After all, one staff breakfast will be good, but turning it into a routine in your school will help you get further toward your goal of building friendly connections among staff.

Finally, a good goal is small enough to be realistic. In his book *Atomic Habits*, James Clear (2018, pp. 13–15) tells a compelling story about the British cycling team that, after a century of mediocrity, became one of the most successful cycling programs in the world. Their key to success? Instead of trying to overhaul the whole program, the coach focused on making small changes. They redesigned bike seats to make them more comfortable, tested various pillows to see which ones gave riders a slightly better night's sleep, painted the interiors of the vans that transported bikes white so that it was easier to see (and clean up) dust that could affect bikes' performances, and so on. Within a few years, they went on a 10-year run as the most accomplished cycling team in the world.

This is important. Big changes tend to be disruptive and are incredibly hard to follow through on. If you're not currently working out at all, walking for 15 minutes three days a week is much more realistic than aiming to go to the gym for an hour five days a week. It might feel heroically exciting to take on big goals ("I'm going to gamify my entire curriculum!"), but a more modest goal that you can actually meet ("I'm going to play one content-based game with my students each Friday") will do you and your students a lot more good in the long run.

Step 2: Use Practical Strategies to Help You Set a New Habit

Willpower is finite and overrated. If you're planning on just forcing yourself to change, good luck. In their fascinating book, *Willpower*, psychologist Roy Baumeister and writer John Tierney (2011) explore self-control in great depth. They highlight how hard it is to force your-self to do something that's new or hard, especially as you get hungry, tired, or make multiple decisions (among other factors)—all things that teachers experience every day. If we overrely on willpower to "make ourselves" change, we're in trouble.

When I share with people that I run for exercise, I often hear, "Wow. I could never do that. I just don't have the willpower to run." In fact, I don't have particularly strong willpower, either. (Just watch me try to walk past a bag of potato chips without eating some, or all, of them.) When I first started to run consistently in my early 40s, it was really hard to get myself out the door. Even once I was running, it was hard not to stop and walk. Now, 10 years later, I've got some habits around running that make it easy to keep going. I had to exercise some willpower to shift into new habits, but now that I'm there, running just happens. I also used (and still use) some concrete strategies to keep me motivated and on track. I record every run in a running journal and tally my miles at the end of each week. I make playlists and listen to music to keep running enjoyable. (My latest is a compilation of songs from musicals. When a cabinet meeting from *Hamilton* came on yesterday, I couldn't help but smile and pick up the pace.) I've signed up for a running group. I don't join as often as I'd like, but they meet every Tuesday, so I know I've got a group if I want one.

We need to not rely on willpower alone as we work at changing habits or forming new ones. We need concrete and practical strategies. And one of the beauties of habits is that once they're formed, they pretty much run on their own, with little or no willpower needed. Although getting into the habit of running was challenging, especially at first, now that it's part of my daily routine, it's almost hard *not* to run.

Step 3: Set a Timeline for When to Check in and Reassess

When will you check your progress? This is an important step. Even if you plan on walking every day and don't plan to stop, you should set a specific date to check in on how you're doing. At that point, you can reas-sess. Is this habit still working? Or is it time to adjust?

Perhaps you decided to offer students more choice in math and set a goal of adding choice in once a week. It might be that after a couple of months, you're successful, and it's not so hard. In fact, it feels like a habit, and it no longer requires any real effort. Congratulations! It might be time to move on. You might up the ante and try giving choice two or three days a week. Or maybe it would be better to shift gears and try a goal in a different area.

It might also be that even though you thought the goal was a good one and was realistic, you're just not able to meet it. Instead of feeling guilty and letting it fade away quietly, be intentional. Take the goal off your plate and try something new.

Specific Strategies for Changing Habits

Throughout this book, you have explored many different possible ideas for changes you might play with in several key categories: foundational needs, competence, purpose, autonomy, curiosity, belonging, and fun. The following strategies might help your new habits stick. These are ideas for how to make a plan that doesn't rely on willpower. Clearly, all these strategies won't work for every habit you might want to change. Pick a few that will help with the specific goal you're taking on.

Post Your Goal in a Visible Place

One of the hardest things about shifting habits, at least at first, is that habits are often unconscious—that is, they're habitual. We slide back into old routines because we're thinking about something else, and the new habit hasn't become automatic yet.

An antidote to this challenge is to post your goal in visible places so that it's brought to your conscious attention more often. Let's say you want to incorporate more intentional gratitude practice into your day. Place a note on the monitor of your computer so that every morning when you come to school, there's a visible reminder: "Name five things for which you're grateful this morning." Or you're planning to listen to podcasts during your commute to get new ideas for teaching and stay abreast of education news and trends. You could put a daily reminder on your phone or place a sticky note on the dashboard of your car. Then, every time you get into your car, the reminder is right there in front of you.

Buddy Up

Getting into new habits is hard, and it can help to have company. Is there someone else who might like to join you in the mentor training program you're planning to sign up for? Having other people who are counting on you to be in a certain place and a certain time can help you stay true to your goal.

In the ADHD community, there's a practice known as body doubling. People who are struggling with getting a task done find ways to do the task with others. They might go to a coffee shop or library to write. They might exercise at a community pool where others are swimming for exercise. The idea is to put yourself in the midst of other people who are doing similar tasks, and their energy rubs off on you. There are productivity apps you might check out where you sign up to work alongside someone else. Some are even using certain social media platforms. They'll livestream themselves doing the dishes or cleaning a closet. Having an audience (and often others who decide to join in) makes the challenging task easier to accomplish.

Try Habit Stacking

Clear (2018) offers this strategy in *Atomic Habits*, and it's one of the most impactful and practical strategies you'll find. The idea here is to stack a new habit onto an existing one.

One of the blessings (and curses) of our profession is that we have strict schedules. While it might feel confining to live by the clock all day, we can also leverage these strict schedules to our advantage. Does every day end with bus duty at 3:15? Put on your sneakers before heading down to bus duty, and as soon as you wave the last bus goodbye, walk laps around the school for 15 minutes. Now getting some exercise has been stacked on top of bus duty, and it's easier to follow through. Are you looking to get a book group going to increase positive time with colleagues and spark new ideas in the classroom? Stack the book group meeting on top of staff meeting days. You're already staying late every other Wednesday, so tack on an extra 30 minutes to discuss a book you're reading. Perhaps you want to dig into an independent action research project but are worried about carving out the time. What if you got to school 20 minutes earlier (or stayed 20 minutes later) each day and devoted that extra time to your personal PD quest? Stack this habit on your entry or exit from the classroom. When I was still in the classroom, I wanted to do some professional writing but was struggling to get to it. I stacked it on top of my morning swim routine. I set the alarm a bit earlier and did a short amount of writing each day before I got in the car to head to the pool, which was a habit stacked on my morning commute. After months of this habit, I had a working draft of my first professional book.

Use Your Calendar to Create Nonnegotiables

Why do we write down IEP meetings and open house night in our calendar but not yoga or family time? We place items on a calendar to remind us as they approach but also to make sure we don't double-book. One way to prioritize personal balance and help get into new routines is to value our personal time as we do our work time. Want to carve out no-work Saturdays? Block the time off and make it a recurring event. Did friends invite you to take a three-day weekend in late October? Make sure to block the personal day off well in advance, before you accidentally agree to chaperone the Fall Formal. You might consider using a specific color (I use yellow) to show personal time saved on your calendar.

You might also consider how to use your calendar to reinforce a new habit you're solidifying. Let's say you're working at taking online asynchronous courses once every two months to boost your sense of curiosity around new teaching strategies. If the first course you're working on takes a total of six hours, find 12 half-hour blocks of time on your calendar and write them in. You might even schedule 15 blocks so you have three you can skip if something else comes up.

Leverage Your Need for Instant Gratification

One of the greatest challenges of focusing on small habit changes is that there's a delay in the rewards we experience. In fact, you might never actually see or feel the difference. For example, if you shift from putting two teaspoons of sugar in your morning tea to one, the compounding effect of this change is huge. One teaspoon of sugar in two cups of tea a day, multiplied over a 30-year span is a staggering 21,900 teaspoons of sugar (roughly 40 five-pound bags)! Of course, you'll be a healthier person not ingesting an extra 40 bags of sugar, but will you actually see or feel the difference on any given day? Probably not. When you don't see an immediate payoff, it can be hard to feel the glow of success that helps keep you motivated to stick with the change.

So when taking on a new habit—especially one that involves small changes—consider a mechanism for tracking your success. Make it visible. For example, keeping a food log is a way to track the foods you are (and aren't) eating. When you write down what you eat each day, it's easier to see your good choices piling up.

That's just one example, of course. You might try the following:

- Mark a tally on a notecard each time you make a proactive positive phone call to a family.

- Write down one small success at the end of each day in a notebook.

- Text a friend "I did it" each time you have a bowl of fruit instead of a bowl of ice cream.

- Create a checklist each week to help you remember to have a private chat with each student and check them off after the conversation.

Play with Math: The Power of Accumulation

Were you a little blown away by the fact that two teaspoons of sugar a day adds up to 40 five-pound bags of sugar in 30 years? This leads us to another strategy that can help with your day-to-day motivation. Pay attention to the power of accumulation. We know this is why saving a small amount of money each month in a retirement account is so powerful. A little bit of money tucked away on a monthly basis will grow into a sizeable nest egg over many years.

The same is true for other small habits that pile up over time. A mile and a half of walking every day after school over a 30-year career (1.5 miles × 180 days × 30 years) yields 8,100 miles. Reading one professional book every two months adds up to 180 books read during that same time period. While walking a mile and a half every afternoon or reading a book every couple of months might not seem like a lot in the moment, they sure do stack up in a sizeable way over time!

As you're planning your new habit, you might want to play around with a similar math exercise to help yourself see the benefits you'll gain in the long run with your new small change.

Take Care of Two Birds with One Stone

Setting small goals also implies that we shouldn't take on more than one goal at a time. Too many changes at once will be overwhelming. However, you might find that one change could hit several needs or categories at once. For example, starting a lunch-bunch group for students who want to eat with you in the classroom each Friday might boost your sense of connection to students (belonging and fun), and these improved relationships might help you be more successful with some kids who are having a tough time, fueling your sense of purpose and boosting your sense of competence. Or perhaps you'd like to get some more exercise and connect more with positive colleagues. You might start a yoga group with a few school friends a couple of days a week. Meet in the gym right after kids leave and put on a YouTube yoga routine. Or you could strengthen your sense of purpose while also reenergizing your creativity by setting a goal to plan one brand-new unit for the upcoming term. Take a unit from a program that you know kids don't love and rework it to make it better align with your vision for what great teaching and learning should look like and what you know your students want and need.

Be Cautious About Rewarding Yourself with Extra Incentives

While jotting down a daily accomplishment (clearing email, planning for 30 minutes, etc.) can feel rewarding, it might feel even more motivational if you add an extra incentive—a small prize for meeting your daily habit goal. For example, a friend of mine was working at writing a book, and he was struggling to force himself to write. We were both presenting at a professional conference for a week, and he wanted to get a bit of writing done each night. He's a huge baseball fan and collects baseball cards, so he bought five packs of baseball cards, one for each night of the conference. After he wrote for 30 minutes each night, he'd reward himself with opening a pack of cards. It worked! He got in his writing each night.

On the one hand, giving yourself a small reward each time you skip chips, play an academic game with students, or write a blog post might seem to make sense. It will boost your motivation, and it's a way to satisfy your need for immediate gratification. But is this a good idea? Are there any potential downsides?

My suggestion is that if you're going to use this kind of motivational strategy, do so sparingly. As I write about in *Tackling the Motivation Crisis*, this kind of reward system can work in the short term, but if you overrely on this strategy and use it for long-term motivation, it can backfire. For one thing, the effect of the reward fades over time. Playing a quick game on your phone as a reward for assessing student work each evening won't feel as fun a month down the road. Focusing on the reward of playing the video game will also draw your focus away from your true goal—to boost your senses of competence and purpose through using daily assessment to inform instruction. Also, adding a reward system to your plan adds complexity, making it potentially harder to follow through on your plan. If you need to reward yourself with a nice walk around the block after you make a few parent phone calls, what do you do if it's raining?

So my suggestion is to avoid the use of self-imposed incentive systems except in rare and short-term instances.

Shape Your Environment to Support Your New Habit

You probably already know why supermarkets and convenience stores place candy and magazines right near registers. We didn't go into the store to get those things, but when they're right in front of us, they're hard to resist.

Whether we like to admit it or not, our behaviors are often shaped by our environment. We grab a handful of M&Ms out of the candy jar that's sitting on the counter. We get onto the elevator in a hotel because it's right by the front desk and the stairs are down the hallway. We check our phone too frequently because it's right in our pocket.

Let's use this tendency to do what's right in front of us to our advantage. Can you think of how you might shape your environment so that it lines up with the new habits you're trying to create? Place healthy snacks such as fruit and nuts on your counter and put cookies and chips in a hard-to-reach part of the cabinet (or don't buy them at all). Put your alarm clock across the room so that you have to get up to turn it off. Hang your personal kudos-of-the-day journal on the wall by your desk so that it's easy to access at the end of each day. Take that social media app that you're trying not to visit so often off your phone or bury it in a folder on the last page of apps so that it's harder to get to. Post a list of different games you've played with students on a chart in a central location in your classroom so that it's right in front of you. I often suggest to teachers who are working to shift a language habit to place sentence starters—examples of the language they're trying to use more often—on posters around their classrooms.

The key to shaping your environment to your benefit is to find small ways of making the things you want to do easier and the things you want to avoid harder.

Pick a Good Time to Change

There's no time like the present. If you have an idea of a habit you'd like to change, why wait? Especially if this habit doesn't involve lots of moving parts, go for it and jump right in. You're going to get in a few extra steps by parking on the far side of the parking lot? Start tomorrow.

If this habit is going to require a bit of extra motivation, or if it's going to involve a more significant shift in your daily or weekly routine, you might want to wait for a more opportune time to make the shift.

Katy Milkman, award-winning behavioral scientist and author of *How to Change,* suggests leveraging what she calls the "fresh start effect" (2021, pp. 18–23). Look for times that signal a fresh start in your routine, and you're more likely to be able to make a change that sticks. Monday mornings or the first day of a new month are examples of fresh starts. Of course, everyone is familiar with the potential of fresh starts of your birthday or January 1.

Our school schedules provide us with other potential fresh starts. We get the benefit of a blank slate and a fresh start at the beginning of each school year, and this is a fantastic time to make a change for the better. We might also tap into fresh starts offered after school vacations or at the beginning of a new quarter, trimester, or semester. We could even use fresh starts offered by the beginning of a new academic unit or after we complete report cards or parent-teacher conferences.

If you're planning to sing more with your 1st graders to boost their engagement and your fun, what if you collected songs over the next few weeks and started the new routine of singing twice a week at the beginning of next month? If you're planning on having colleagues share games and activities with others at staff meetings, send out the email invitation and start with the staff meeting at the beginning of the next marking period.

Fake It 'Til You Make It

There's a good chance that when you work at reshaping a habit or forming a new one, it will feel unnatural. You might even experience a bit of imposter syndrome. (I'm not really a runner. I'm not really a teacher who cracks jokes. I'm not really a writer.) This is normal and natural. Of course you're going to feel uncomfortable as you try to change some habits! It would be weird if you didn't. When I first started wearing a tie to school to boost my sense of professionalism, it felt odd at first. After a few weeks, it didn't feel so strange. Now, it would feel odd if I went to school without a tie.

Sometimes, it's helpful to follow some age-old advice: fake it 'til you make it. We all eventually become what we pretend to be. New waiters pretend to be waiters until they feel like waiters. New lifeguards pretend to be lifeguards until they feel like lifeguards.

Changing habits can sometimes involve changing our self-perception. Decide what change you'd like to make, and fake your way to a habit that will make a real difference over time.

Fires Need Tending

One of our family's favorite areas of our house is the family room in front of the woodstove. From October through March, this is where we spend most of our time. It's cozy to hunker down in front of the fire as cold rain or snow comes down outside.

In the morning, I start the fire with lots of paper and kindling to get a nice hot blaze going. A strong fire early helps establish a base of coals to keep the stove going throughout the day.

Even with the base of coals, though, the fire needs attention. You have to be careful not to keep the fire too bright for too long. The house can get overly warm, and if the fire's hot enough, it can damage the stove. (I learned this the hard way with our previous stove that was too small for the room. I kept it so hot that the back of the stove cracked.) On the other hand, if you ignore the fire for too long, it gets too cool to accept new wood. You have to start all over again, which wastes paper and kindling. It also takes a lot more time and attention to restart the fire once it's out.

Instead, the fire needs to be tended regularly throughout the day. The fire burns bright and hot early and then settles into a slow burn. Every couple of hours, you have to add a bit more wood. Sometimes a few smaller pieces are best. They help the fire flare quickly if it's getting too low. Sometimes a larger one is better for a long slow burn. Perhaps a medium-size piece might be enough. With on-again off-again attention, you can keep a steady fire going without much time and effort.

Isn't this the same for our professional energy during a school year? The beginning of the year almost always burns bright and hot. Our energy and enthusiasm are high, but it's not realistic for the fire to stay at that level throughout the year. Sometimes we've got a steady, even flame, and other times our fire burns a little lower and cooler.

We have to be careful, though, that we don't ignore our own professional fires for too long. If they cool too much, they're hard to restart. Instead, just as with an actual fire, some periodic tending is required. Sometimes, a fresh jolt of belonging or curiosity might do the trick. Perhaps a boost of autonomy or competence is required. With a little tending, you can keep your professional fire burning not just throughout the year, but year after year.

Are You Ready to Make a Plan?

With that in mind, are you ready to craft a plan—one that will actually work? Remember, it's not selfish to engage in self-care. Your students need and deserve teachers who are fired up, energized, and excited to come to school each day. Your family and friends will benefit if you are healthy and positively engaged. Use the following template (see Figure 6.1) and sample guide (see Figure 6.2) to help you map out your plan.

Figure 6.1 Planning Guide Template

It can be overwhelming to consider making a change—even if you know it will be beneficial in the long run. This guide will help you clarify possible goals and find a good starting point.

Generate Some Possibilities: In the spaces below, jot some ideas from each chapter that resonated for you. Which ideas might you want to try? It's fine (even encouraged) to write down lots of possibilities, including ones you probably won't tackle just yet. You'll sharpen your focus later.

Chapter 2: Recharge Your Battery	Chapter 3: Recover Your Swagger
Chapter 4: Rekindle Your Professional Fire	**Chapter 5: Refresh Your Spirit**

Chapter 6: How to Build Powerful Hew Habits

Step 1: Create a Good Goal

Look at the possibilities you generated. Do any seem to go together? Is there a big theme or category that seems especially important?

Think of a specific and concrete goal that might help address that big theme or category. Make sure that it's small enough of a goal that it will be achievable and not overwhelming. If possible, make the goal about a habit you want to change or adopt—not a one-time event.

My goal is . . .

Step 2: Use Practical Strategies to Help You Set a New Habit

What is a practical strategy or two that will help you follow through on your goal? Use suggestions on pages 107–114 for inspiration.

I'll use these strategies . . .

Step 3: Set a Timeline for When to Check in and Reassess

When will you check in and reflect on how your goal is coming along? Consider making this date not too far in the future. Put a reminder on your calendar so that you don't forget!

I'll check on progress on . . .

Step 4: Return to Step 1

Once you have solidified your new habit (congratulations!), you can return to the beginning of the planning process to begin anew.

Figure 6.2 Planning Guide Example

It can be overwhelming to consider making a change—even if you know it will be beneficial in the long run. This guide will help you clarify possible goals and find a good starting point.

Generate Some Possibilities: In the spaces below, jot some ideas from each chapter that resonated for you. Which ideas might you want to try? It's fine (even encouraged) to write down lots of possibilities, including ones you probably won't tackle just yet. You'll sharpen your focus later.

Chapter 2: Recharge Your Battery	Chapter 3: Recover Your Swagger
• Keep almonds and raisins in classroom • Bring walking shoes to school, walk with friends in afternoon on trails behind school • Maybe start an after-school walking club?	• Like the idea of writing a mission/vision statement • Every day, write down a few positives • Are there any responsibilities I could let go of?
Chapter 4: **Rekindle Your Professional Fire**	**Chapter 5:** **Refresh Your Spirit**
• Love the idea of reworking some units in literacy program, but not sure where to start • My classroom could definitely use a makeover...maybe next semester	• After-school walking club would boost belonging and healthy activity • Suggest math mornings in place of "donuts with dad" to principal • Crabs in a bucket, ha! • I could use more gratitude in my life right now...

Chapter 6: How to Build Powerful Hew Habits

Step 1: Create a Good Goal

Look at the possibilities you generated. Do any seem to go together? Is there a big theme or category that seems especially important?

Think of a specific and concrete goal that might help address that big theme or category. Make sure that it's small enough of a goal that it will be achievable and not overwhelming. If possible, make the goal about a habit you want to change or adopt—not a one-time event.

> My goal is . . .
>
> to reset my afternoon routine to get in some more movement and positive energy before I head home
>
> New routine:
> - Walk for 20 minutes after students are dismissed
> - Invite others to join—and be transparent that the goal is to share positives from the day—to feel good before heading home
> - Wrap in positives and gratitudes

Step 2: Use Practical Strategies to Help You Set a New Habit

What is a practical strategy or two that will help you follow through on your goal? Use suggestions on pages 107–114 for inspiration.

> I'll use these strategies . . .
>
> - Start a health journal to help with self-accountability
>   - Record minutes walked each day
>   - Record two successes and one thing I'm grateful for each afternoon
> - Habit stacking: write down two successes and one thing I'm grateful for in a journal right after I put on my sneakers before walk
> - Keep health journal in a visible spot in room, right near my walking shoes
> - Add this new routine to my calendar to help get the new habit formed

Step 3: Set a Timeline for When to Check in and Reassess

When will you check in and reflect on how your goal is coming along? Consider making this date not too far in the future. Put a reminder on your calendar so that you don't forget!

> I'll check on progress on . . .
>
> - I'll check on this habit in one month to see how it's going. I might be able to remove reminders from my calendar. I might also adjust the number of minutes I'm walking, depending on how it's going.

Step 4: Return to Step 1

Once you have solidified your new habit (congratulations!), you can return to the beginning of the planning process to begin anew.

Acknowledgments

Why do we so often have kids engage in school writing as a solo endeavor? They're supposed to think of ideas to write on their own, create rough drafts by themselves, and even edit their writing solo. That's not how real writing usually works. Initial ideas are crafted in collaboration with others, revisions happen after pushes and questions from peers, and editors help refine ideas and catch mistakes. Sure, there are plenty of long hours alone at the computer, but I've never written a book by myself. This one was certainly no exception.

There were many colleagues who helped me think through elements of this book as it was in process. Thanks, Erin Moore, for helping me keep my eye on the ball early on. You might not realize how your gentle push in the early stages guided my thinking for much of the book. Thanks also to Pete Hall, Chris Hall (no relation!), Erin Jones, and Tom Tuscano for letting me share some of your wisdom and experiences with others.

Heather, my wife, was also instrumental in bringing this book to life. She endured (and I hope sometimes enjoyed) impromptu writing conferences as I struggled with an idea. Her own experiences as a teacher, first as a 2nd grade teacher and now as a knitting instructor for adults, offered new insights for me as I played with ideas. Plus, she's just generally an awesome person, which makes writing and life better most days.

How is it that I can think about a book idea for months, drafting multiple essays and chapters, and with one short call, Genny Ostertag can help pull everything together? I don't need to understand to appreciate. Once again, Genny, thank you so much for your guidance and support.

And to Liz Wegner, thanks for saving me from the perils of too many exclamation points and dashes. You always help me sound smarter and more refined than I am (—clearly!). Thanks also to the whole ASCD team. Your never-ending quest to help education be better for all kids is inspirational and much appreciated!

References

Adam, H., & Galinsky, A. D. (2012). Enclothed cognition. *Journal of Experimental Social Psychology, 48*(4), 918–925.

Anderson, M. (2016). *Learning to choose, choosing to learn: The key to student motivation and achievement.* ASCD.

Anderson, M. (2021). *Tackling the motivation crisis: How to activate student learning without behavior charts, pizza parties, or other hard-to-quit incentive systems.* ASCD.

Aronofsky, D., Handel, A. (Writers), Robinson, K. L., & Jens Schillmöller, J. (Directors). (2022, November 16). Memory (Season 1, Episode 5) [TV series episode]. In D. Aronofsky, B. Grayson, C. Hemsworth, J. Root, A. Nurmohamed, & A. Handel (Executive Producers), *Limitless.* National Geographic; Nutopia; Protozoa Pictures; Wild State.

Asl, R. G., Taghinejad, R., Parizad, N., & Jasemi, M. (2022). The relationship between professional autonomy and job stress among intensive care unit nurses: A descriptive correlational study. *Iranian Journal of Nursing and Midwifery Research, 27*(2), 119.

Aydin, E., & Azizoğlu, Ö. (2022, October 7–9). *A new term for an existing concept: Quiet quitting—A self-determination perspective* [Conference paper]. V. International Critical Debates in Social Sciences Congress. https://www.researchgate.net/publication/366530514

Baumeister, R. F., & Tierney, J. (2011). *Willpower: Rediscovering the greatest human strength.* Penguin.

Bratman, G. N., Daily, G. C., Levy, B. J., & Gross, J. J. (2015). The benefits of nature experience: Improved affect and cognition. *Landscape and Urban Planning, 138*, 41–50.

Bryant, J., & Zillmann, D. (2014). Using humor to promote learning in the classroom. *Humor and children's development: A guide to practical applications*, 49–78.

Buettner, D., Jeter, C., Kubena, K., & Wall, A. (Executive Producers). (2023). *Live to 100: Secrets of the blue zones* [TV series]. MakeMake Entertainment.

Centers for Disease Control and Prevention. (2022, September 19). Are you getting enough sleep? https://www.cdc.gov/sleep/features/getting-enough-sleep.html

Clear, J. (2018). *Atomic habits: An easy and proven way to build good habits and break bad ones*. Penguin.

Cordes, C. L., & Dougherty, T. W. (1993). A review and an integration of research on job burnout. *Academy of Management Review, 18*(4), 621–656.

Cross, M. P., Acevedo, A. M., Leger, K. A., & Pressman, S. D. (2022). How and why could smiling influence physical health? A conceptual review. *Health Psychology Review*, 1–23.

Deci, E. L., & Flaste, R. (1995). *Why we do what we do: Understanding self-motivation*. Putnam's.

DeWitt, P. M. (2022). *De-implementation: Creating the space to focus on what works*. Corwin.

Donohoo, J., Hattie, J., & Eells, R. (2018). The power of collective efficacy. *Educational Leadership, 75*(6), 40–44. https://www.ascd.org/el/articles/the-power-of -collective-efficacy

Duhigg, C. (2013). *The power of habit: Why we do what we do and how to change*. Random House.

Glass, D. C., & McKnight, J. D. (1996). Perceived control, depressive symptomatology, and professional burnout: A review of the evidence. *Psychology and Health, 11*(1), 23–48.

Guéguen, N., & De Gail, M. A. (2003). The effect of smiling on helping behavior: Smiling and good Samaritan behavior. *Communication Reports, 16*(2), 133–140.

Hall, C. (2021). *The writer's mindset: Six stances that promote authentic revision*. Heinemann.

Hambleton, B. (2021, October 20). Eliud Kipchoge running SLOW on his easy day. *Running*. https://runningmagazine.ca/sections/training/watch-eliud-kipchoge -running-slow-on-his-easy-day/

Harris, D. (2014). *10% happier: How I tamed the voice in my head, reduced stress without losing my edge, and found self-help that actually works—a true story*. Hachette UK.

Harvard Health Publishing. (2021, August 14). Giving thanks can make you happier. https://www.health.harvard.edu/healthbeat/giving-thanks-can-make-you -happier

Hatfield, E., Cacioppo, J. T., & Rapson, R. L. (1993). Emotional contagion. *Current Directions in Psychological Science, 2*(3), 96–100.

Herrando, C., & Constantinides, E. (2021). Emotional contagion: A brief overview and future directions. *Frontiers in Psychology, 12*, 2881.

Heubeck, E. (2024, January 24). One school district just pulled 1,600 books from its shelves—including the dictionary. *Education Week*. https://www.edweek.org/ teaching-learning/one-school-district-just-pulled-1-600-books-from-its -shelves-including-the-dictionary/2024/01

Jones, E. (2021). *Bridges to heal us: Stories and strategies for racial healing*.

Kadey, M. (2023, August 30). 5 packaged foods that offer energy and nutrients for your runs. https://www.runnersworld.com/nutrition-weight-loss/a44951757/ best-packaged-foods/

Kasalak, G., & Dagyar, M. (2020). The relationship between teacher self-efficacy and teacher job satisfaction: A meta-analysis of the teaching and learning international survey (TALIS). *Educational Sciences: Theory and Practice, 20*(3), 16–33.

Kwon, Y. H. (1994). The influence of appropriateness of dress and gender on the self-perception of occupational attributes. *Clothing and Textiles Research Journal, 12*(3), 33–39.

Lackey, N. Q., Tysor, D. A., McNay, G. D., Joyner, L., Baker, K. H., & Hodge, C. (2021). Mental health benefits of nature-based recreation: A systematic review. *Annals of Leisure Research, 24*(3), 379–393.

Louv, R. (2008). *Last child in the woods: Saving our children from nature-deficit disorder*. Algonquin Books.

Marmolejo-Ramos, F., Murata, A., Sasaki, K., Yamada, Y., Ikeda, A., Hinojosa, J. A., Watanabe, K., Parzuchowski, M., Tirado, C., & Ospina, R. (2020). Your face and moves seem happier when I smile: Facial action influences the perception of emotional faces and biological motion stimuli. *Experimental Psychology, 67*(1), 14–22.

Maslach, C. (2011). Burnout and engagement in the workplace: New perspectives. *European Health Psychologist, 13*(3), 44–47.

Maslow, A. H. (1943). A theory of human motivation. *Psychological Review, 50*(4), 370–396.

Michael Jr. (2017). *Know your why* [Video]. https://www.youtube.com/watch?v=1ytFB8TrkTo

Milkman, K. (2021). *How to change: The science of getting from where you are to where you want to be*. Penguin.

Mitra, S. (2010, July). *The child driven education* [Video]. TEDGlobal 2010. https://www.ted.com/talks/sugata_mitra_the_child_driven_education?language=en

Pearson, L. C., & Moomaw, W. (2005). The relationship between teacher autonomy and stress, work satisfaction, empowerment, and professionalism. *Educational Research Quarterly, 29*(1), 38–54.

Pollan, M. (2009). *In defense of food: An eater's manifesto*. Penguin.

Savage, B. M., Lujan, H. L., Thipparthi, R. R., & DiCarlo, S. E. (2017). Humor, laughter, learning, and health! A brief review. *Advances in physiology education*.

Spector, P. E. (1986). Perceived control by employees: A meta-analysis of studies concerning autonomy and participation at work. *Human Relations, 39*(11), 1005–1016.

Taylor, J. (2023, February 9). Smiling is a powerful mental tool for endurance athletes. https://www.psychologytoday.com/us/blog/the-power-of-prime/202302/smiling-is-a-powerful-mental-tool-for-endurance-athletes

Tschannen-Moran, M., & Woolfork, A. (2001.) Teacher efficacy: Capturing an elusive construct. *Teaching and Teacher Education, 17*(7), 783–805.

Walker, M. (n.d.). *Matthew Walker teaches the science of better sleep*. MasterClass. https://www.masterclass.com/classes/matthew-walker-teaches-the-science-of-better-sleep

Walker, T. D. (2017). *Teach like Finland: 33 simple strategies for joyful classrooms*. Norton.

Watta, E. (2022, September 25). Eliud Kipchoge breaks the world record at the 2022 Berlin marathon. *Olympics.* https://olympics.com/en/news/eliud-kipchoge-new-mens-world-record-2022-berlin-marathon

Welteroth, E. (n.d.). *Elaine Welteroth teaches designing your career.* MasterClass. https://www.masterclass.com/classes/elaine-welteroth-teaches-designing-your-career

Wilfong, S., & Donlan, R. (2021). How mattering matters for educators. *Educational Leadership, 79*(3), 51–56. https://www.ascd.org/el/articles/how-mattering-matters-for-educators

Yousafzai, M. (n.d.). *Malala teaches creating change.* MasterClass. https://www.masterclass.com/classes/malala-yousafzai-teaches-creating-change/

Ziv, A. (1988). Teaching and learning with humor: Experiment and replication. *Journal of Experimental Education, 57*(1), 4–15.

Index

The letter *f* following a page locator denotes a figure.

About the Author

Mike Anderson has been an educator for many years. A classroom teacher for 15 years, he has also coached swim teams, worked in preschools, and taught university graduate-level classes. In 2004, Anderson was awarded a national Milken Educator Award, and in 2005, he was a finalist for New Hampshire Teacher of the Year.

Now an independent education consultant, Anderson works with schools in rural, urban, and suburban settings across the United States and beyond. Anderson supports teachers and schools on a wide variety of topics: boosting student motivation, using effective teacher talk, embedding choice in everyday learning, blending social-emotional and academic teaching, and many more. It is his firm belief that professional learning should be engaging and joyful and should model what great classroom teaching is all about. In 2020, he was awarded the Outstanding Educational Leader Award by NHASCD for his work as a consultant.

Anderson is the author of many books about great teaching and learning including *The Research-Ready Classroom* (Heinemann, 2006), *The Well-Balanced Teacher* (ASCD, 2010), *The First Six Weeks of School,* 2nd Edition (CRS, 2015), *Tackling the Motivation Crisis* (ASCD, 2021), and the bestselling *What We Say and How We Say It Matter* (ASCD, 2019).

Anderson lives in Durham, New Hampshire, with his amazing family: Heather, Ethan, and Carly (though with Ethan and Carly in the process of fledging, this is very much in flux). When he's not working, you might find him tending his perennial gardens, watching the Red Sox, or finding fun new places to run.

To learn more about Anderson and his work, visit his website: www .leadinggreatlearning.com. Through that site you can read his blog, subscribe to his newsletter, and learn about the many online courses he has created for teachers. You can also follow him on Twitter/X at @balancedteacher.

Related ASCD Resources

At the time of publication, the following resources were available (ASCD stock numbers in parentheses).

Building Teacher Capacity Through Reflection (Quick Reference Guide) by Pete Hall & Alisa Simeral (#QRG117099)

The Burnout Cure: Learning to Love Teaching Again by Chase Mielke (#119004)

Educator Bandwidth: How to Reclaim Your Energy, Passion, and Time by Jane Kise & Ann Holm (#122019)

Illuminate the Way: The School Leader's Guide to Addressing and Preventing Teacher Burnout by Chase Mielke (#123032)

Make Teaching Sustainable: Six Shifts That Teachers Want and Students Need by Paul Emerich France (#123011)

Manage Your Time or Time Will Manage You: Strategies That Work from an Educator Who's Been There by PJ Caposey (#119005)

The Minimalist Teacher by Tamera Musiowsky-Borneman & C. Y. Arnold (#121058)

Overcoming Educator Burnout (Quick Reference Guide) by Chase Mielke (#QRG123016)

Tackling the Motivation Crisis: How to Activate Student Learning Without Behavior Charts, Pizza Parties, or Other Hard-to-Quit Incentive Systems by Mike Anderson (#121033)

The Teacher 50: Critical Questions for Inspiring Classroom Excellence by Baruti K. Kafele (#117009)

Teach Happier This School Year: 40 Weeks of Inspiration and Reflection by Suzanne Dailey (#123027)

Teach, Reflect, Learn: Building Your Capacity for Success in the Classroom by Pete Hall & Alisa Simeral (#115040)

What Can I Take Off Your Plate? A Structural—and Sustainable—Approach to Countering Teacher Burnout by Jill Handley & Lara Donnelly (#125002)

For up-to-date information about ASCD resources, go to www.ascd.org. You can search the complete archives of *Educational Leadership* at www.ascd.org/el. To contact us, send an email to member@ascd.org or call 1-800-933-2723 or 703-578-9600.

WHOLE CHILD
TENETS

The ASCD Whole Child approach is an effort to transition from a focus on narrowly defined academic achievement to one that promotes the long-term development and success of all children. Through this approach, ASCD supports educators, families, community members, and policymakers as they move from a vision about educating the whole child to sustainable, collaborative actions.

Rekindle Your Professional Fire relates to the **healthy** tenet.

For more about the ASCD Whole Child approach, visit **www.ascd.org/wholechild.**

1 HEALTHY
Each student enters school healthy and learns about and practices a healthy lifestyle.

2 SAFE
Each student learns in an environment that is physically and emotionally safe for students and adults.

3 ENGAGED
Each student is actively engaged in learning and is connected to the school and broader community.

4 SUPPORTED
Each student has access to personalized learning and is supported by qualified, caring adults.

5 CHALLENGED
Each student is challenged academically and prepared for success in college or further study and for employment and participation in a global environment.